T0209097

MADE BEAUTIFUL
BY SCARS

MADE BEAUTIFUL
BY SCARS
REAL WOMEN'S STORIES

VERONICA FARMER

BALBOA.
PRESS

A DIVISION OF HAY HOUSE

Balboa Press books may be ordered through booksellers or by contacting:

Balboa Press
A Division of Hay House
1663 Liberty Drive
Bloomington, IN 47403
www.balboapress.com.au
1 (877) 407-4847

Because of the dynamic nature of the Internet, any web addresses or links contained in this book may have changed since publication and may no longer be valid. The views expressed in this work are solely those of the author and do not necessarily reflect the views of the publisher, and the publisher hereby disclaims any responsibility for them.

. The author of this book does not dispense medical advice or prescribe the use of any technique as a form of treatment for physical, emotional, or medical problems without the advice of a physician, either directly or indirectly. The intent of the author is only to offer information of a general nature to help you in your quest for emotional and spiritual well-being. In the event you use any of the information in this book for yourself, which is your constitutional right, the author and the publisher assume no responsibility for your actions.

Cover photograph by Chicoz Photography.

Credits to Chicoz Photography, Carolyn Haslett, Kyle George, Hayley Johnson for all interior photographs and Kate Cornfoot Photography for interior and back cover photographs

Print information available on the last page.

ISBN: 978-1-5043-0297-5 (sc)
ISBN: 978-1-5043-0302-6 (e)

Balboa Press rev. date: 07/15/2016

Acknowledgments

Thank you to all who were part of this creation. Thank you to the creative Universal Force who inspired it and to all the brave souls who gave their blood, sweat, and tears to the project. Thank you to the ones I love who put up with me, and thank you, Chicoz Photography, for my playful cover shot!

For the Scarred Ones

For my scarred soul tribe,
You are loved.
Loved.
For you are brave
In your walk through dark places,
Loved for your scars that have made you,
Loved for your shoulders back and head held high,
Loved for the nights your forehead felt
        It would hit the floor.
I thank all those who have shared their pain,
Their tears
And joys
To heal us
And help us know
        We are not alone.
And for those who have lovingly
Helped, held, and
Supported us on our journey,
Had our backs
So we could keep walking
        And writing
Our vulnerable truth
And be healed by it.
We love you
        Very much.
Eshua Lalei.
All is love.

CONTENTS

INTRODUCTION

I have waited thirteen years to write this book. Part of me was waiting for a good distance away from cancer to tell my own story about how I have been made beautiful by that particular life scar.

This book began as an idea to share how cancer made me more beautiful. But as I shared my story with others, I realized how many incredible people around me had been made beautiful by their own great scars. I realized that every one of us is covered with scrapes and scars, and so the book expanded to include these stories by women who had lived through trauma that did not break them. It did something much more than that—it grew them, expanded their beauty into a whole new realm, and touched so many other souls.

My gift of finding health was a scar that turned into a miracle. I was left with the gift of being able to heal not just myself but many others, and I would not change a thing about my walk.

The scar of a broken heart is one many of us explore in our life's journey, along with grief, loss, and disease. These wounds can teach us how to love more, be more, and give more to the world around us. It is the journey of a life richly lived.

In my journey of bringing this book together, I have met some extraordinary women—women who have overcome some truly challenging life scars and been made more glorious as a result. The intention of this book was not to collect tragedies or ever lay blame but to show the amazing nature of women who can go through incredibly painful events, widen their hearts, minds, and ability to connect with the world around them, and inspire us to do the same.

I believe that scars are a normal human expression. Pain and mistakes make you human, and the only way to avoid these is to hide out in a cave. Having bad things happen to you does not make you less, although society tells us to get through our challenges quickly, hide our scars, and put on a happy face. When you walk through the dark nights of the soul, explore all of the feelings and allow time to process and heal. This deep connection with the wounds and scars takes the body, mind, and heart to resolution.

Acceptance helps us move forward so we can share our wisdom with others.

Scars make you, evolve you, create you, and—if given half the chance—heal many others too.

The women in this book are fiercely brave. They have a powerful human spirit that has pushed through and kept on walking. Many have said "No!" to limits others have put on their lives and come up with amazing solutions. I hope they inspire you to do the same.

I have met these women in unusual ways, at unusual times. I have found them or they have found me, and I am profoundly grateful for their brave vulnerability. The people that are mentioned in these stories have been given other names to protect their privacy, and that is one of the reasons we have welcomed stories on this project using just first names. It makes us everyday people, just like you.

I hope you enjoy this book and begin to see how the scars you have worn on your own heart, mind, or body have made you more beautiful, wise, and more loving.

My intention is to value your story, to share your felt wisdom from your own scar experience with the world. So, if you are keen to read more stories like these, of real people just like you, keep connecting with us on Facebook and on our website. We publish excerpts of new stories regularly.

If you have a story swirling in your heart, send it over to www.madebeautifulbyscars.com.

I can't wait to share with you the latest stories by real people who might just offer exactly what you need to hear.

Sound good?

Get writing, my friends!

Let the stories come …

With a pile of love,

Veronica x

Kate Cornfoot Photography

Veronica's Story

Chicoz Photography

SCARS IN THE MIND

I have lived a few lifetimes in these same bones and skin. Each day now feels to me like an entire life—birth to death in one day. My heart is wide and runs deep, inhaling and exhaling connection and love from the air around me and from people I meet. I am forty-seven years old, and never have I felt so profoundly alive, rich in life, and aware of *who I am* as I do now. I could not have gotten here without a boatload of scars on my body, mind, and heart.

My concept of an ideal relationship was cemented deeply in what I had watched and witnessed growing up; the media educated me to believe a relationship should be a fairy tale, that I should aspire to be Cinderella and find my Prince Charming. I was trained to see worthiness in a man if he could provide financially, had a good background, and was well educated. I had grown up with a father who provided and a mother who mothered. If they had problems, only a snapping comment from my father or anxiety and sickness from my mother would show that there were cracks in the framework.

We lived the picket-fence existence, the one many of us are taught to aim for. My parents worked hard buying and renovating homes. My father worked in the airlines and this meant that we travelled the world and had some incredible adventures. My sister and brother and I attended top schools and focused on mind expansion through what university education could offer. We did not do the ideal traditional pathways of my peers—law, medicine, or accounting but arts, history, anthropology, and languages. I completed a Masters degree in History as I was deeply drawn to the past. There was a certain cold aloofness in this space. Here, vulnerability was never shown, but I felt safe and protected in intellectualism. It was a critical life where I looked out from myself at the world and judged all I saw as either okay or not okay.

I was taught by the society in which I lived to find a partner like me. If I did, this ideal model would bring me happiness. Something in me rebelled, though; with everything I had been given in life, I did not know who I was in my own heart. I did not trust emotions. I buried any feelings deep underground. I knew that I did not want to feel controlled and dominated by a partner; I wanted a more easy-going relationship than the one I had witnessed between my parents when I was growing

3

up. I craved a relationship where I did not feel a constant state of anxiety and of competitive debate.

A woman begins to understand who she is between the ages of thirteen and seventeen. She lays down her identity, her belief in herself as a being at that time. I was an awkward, funny-looking redheaded kid. I was the last girl to get her period. I was skinny—and reminded of it constantly by my family. I was nervy but enthusiastic. I desperately wanted to be liked and to fit in, but because I did not have the unfreckled skin and the tamed, glossy hair of my friends, I felt plain; the face I saw in the mirror did not match who I felt I was on the inside.

Then at twenty, I had blossomed without realizing it. I fell in love and began to walk the Yellow Brick Road. I had adhered to the lessons taught during my upbringing and by society: move in together, get married, and have a child and a mortgage. I had a problem within me, though not one I recognized at the time or could share with anyone; it was a real blind spot. I did not trust myself to feel emotions or have any connection with my body other than loathing. At all.

I did not notice if I was hungry or thirsty. I had sex and felt mainly awkward embarrassment. It felt deeply uncomfortable being in my skin. I lived in a constant flurry of anxiety (unless I drank alcohol). I know now that my body was still in trauma from my first sexual experience and that it did not trust being that close to another person's skin.

When I was seventeen, I was a virgin and still very plain in my own eyes. One night, while staying over at a friend's house while her parents were overseas, I awoke to find her brother on top of me. I was the only one home with him. I had been out earlier in the night with his sister, but after watching her and some guy getting it on, I took a cab back to her place and went to bed. Her brother was good-looking and popular, and as he lay on top of me, his weight pinning me down, he told me he thought I was sexy. No one had ever said that to me before, and I was confused. Knowing that was how women were *supposed* to be seen, and as I had always thought I was remarkably average, I didn't know what to do. I became the possum in the headlights as he pulled off my pajamas and forced himself into me.

I did not dare to scream at the pain; this came from a deep disconnection with the body I had always felt. As a small child, as I fell into a half-sleep state, I would feel myself lift, rise, and bump against the ceiling. I could look down on the tiny curled-up body below me, wanting to fly free and get away as far as I could from my body, my life. It was a strange, disconnected existence.

For much of my life, I never quite felt that I belonged here on this planet. Watching the world this way meant that I often did not understand social cues. I was an excellent shape-shifter; I could transform my words, body language, and behavior depending on whom I was with. I adapted as needed, to be liked and to fit in. I think I had such a deep fear of humiliation and embarrassment within me that in avoiding conflict, I allowed others to lead, make decisions, and choose the way forward. I did not know how to find my own center, my own truth, and my own voice.

This disconnection from my body seemed like a normal way to live. It kept me free from feeling and emotional discomfort. I could watch and cast a critical eye around me at the world, and this made me feel safe (although at times I would feel deeply claustrophobic). I wanted to get out of this cage of a body, but I felt *trapped* here.

I am bisexual, and this was not something I could discuss growing up in the 1980s, not with my family, friends, or anyone. I went to an all-girls Catholic school, and my first crush was on one of my young female teachers. I could not make sense of this feeling. As I was so engaged in being both accepted and acceptable, this just didn't allow any room for exploration. More than this, I was defined by the Catholic pain body around sexuality, particularly the fear of homosexuality. I could feel it; I didn't want any part of it. Being bisexual meant that this feeling toward my teacher would make me catch my throat when around her, and at the same time, I felt my heart pound out of my chest when watching Anthony Andrews in *Ivanhoe*. I remember the moment clearly: I was fifteen years old and babysitting. Something about the way he moved made me stand, holding my heart and wondering what was "wrong" with me.

I didn't think I could talk about being attracted to both sexes to my family. I should have been able to, considering my dad worked in the travel industry, and they often held big dress-up parties with lots of shrieking and laughter from the gorgeous gay cabin crew. There was a tightly held pain body in the Catholic world around me about being gay though. For those a generation or two back, there had been so much hidden sexual abuse. As a result, being gay, bisexual, or lesbian was not a free or easy subject to bring up within this backdrop of old Catholic guilt, abuse, and sexual shame.

5

My family and extended family was full of nuns and priests. A grandparent had been a trainee priest before meeting my grandmother, and an aunt is a Carmelite nun in one of the strictest Catholic orders possible. As children, we used to visit her sitting in a freezing room behind a wall of bars like a jail cell. Another great-uncle had been a priest in the Allied army during World War II. He was a clever man who spoke many languages fluently. He had apparently played chess in the African desert with German Field Marshall Erwin Rommel, (aka the Desert Fox), one of the few who was *not* accused of war crimes.

Whispers of hidden sexuality were the norm growing up in this world. I believe now that it is not natural for human beings to curtail sexual energy; it is a powerful, natural human birthright, and if it is not allowed loving, full expression, it goes underground and creates pain.

At the Catholic primary school I attended, as well as in most schools, children were still being caned, hit, and verbally abused. When I was about seven or eight years old, I started at a Catholic primary school when our family moved out of town. At the old state school I had left behind, we were only halfway through learning our mathematics timetables. One afternoon during my first week at this new school, the teacher called me up to the front of the class. When I failed to provide the correct answer to a multiplication question, she slapped me hard across the face and called me a "stupid fool." I ran from the room and hid out for the rest of the day in the toilets. No one came to find me.

When the bell rang, I ran, grabbed my bag, and waited quietly to go home. Because I did not want to expand that overwhelming feeling of humiliation any further or cause problems to a family trying to settle into a new community, I said nothing to my family. The shock of that slap broke something in me. It created a permanent trauma around learning mathematics for me; to this day, I still feel a stab of anxiety when tasked with remembering a series of numbers.

I kept my head down for the rest of the year. We had a beautiful boy in our class who was autistic. I remember how he would sit on the playground and gently watch insects under the trees. Although our classroom was two stories up, the teacher would often hoist him up and shake him headfirst out the window. I can still clearly see his gray, wrinkled socks and shoes kicking with terror and her bulging eyes furious with him. I am sure this left some terrible scars in that child.

Humiliation was a tool well used by the Catholic establishment to control students. In another class a year or so later, we were allowed the privilege of wearing mufti (casual) clothes instead of our standard uniform for a special feast day. My teacher then, a ferocious Irish nun, decided to run a best-dressed competition and paraded each one of us in front of the class to be looked over by our classmates.

She made an example of a child who came from a poorer home. Pointing at her skirt, she said, "How many of your older sisters have worn this hideous garment?" I can still see that child's face red with shame, her eyes glued to the floor.

So, with this backdrop of strong Catholic heritage and hidden guilt, fear, and shame-laden sexuality running deep in the river of my DNA, it made it near impossible to explore that bisexual part of myself that wanted to live outside the realms of the expected behavior.

I did try to talk to my family about being attracted to both sexes once. I was always passionately debating something over the dinner table, usually indigenous rights or women's rights to equal pay. One conversation helped me feel that the topic of sexuality outside the "normal" was not safe. I would have been thirteen years old, and I was in full flow of conversation over gay rights. It wasn't until 1986 that the Homosexual Law Reform Act came into effect, and I was talking about how wrong it was that we were judging people based on who they loved. My point was that if you loved someone, you should be able to walk down the street holding his or her hand. This was 1981, and being gay was illegal in New Zealand. Being a lesbian was not illegal, thanks to Queen Victoria not believing that lesbianism was an actual possibility; however, many lesbians suffered the same social discrimination and derision.

I remember hearing, "You keep talking this way, and you will end up some tough lesbian." For my young self, it was intense to consider that I would be something less than beautiful expressing my full and healthy sexuality, and it made me sure it was going to be a no-go area for me. Shutting that down did some damage around self-trust, sexuality, and body love for a long time.

I believed that the best plan was to follow the fairy tale. Finish university, get an appropriate job, get married, decorate a home, follow the model of choosing a husband who would put on a heavy backpack of expectation and provision, stay tight with the family, be wary of others, have children, and grow old. The problem was that this story that I had learned to believe in was not going to quite work out as planned.

By the time my baby girl was only a few weeks old, I knew I would be leaving. A classic combination of financial pain and exhaustion, breastfeeding while working and my inability to communicate was overwhelming. I left, taking my little girl, and set up a new life with help from my parents, living in a small country cottage and finding a new job and extra help to bring up my child.

Still I felt uneasy, a deep sense of unexplored adventure, of hopes unmet. I was working for a company full of scientists and intellectuals, and we would work hard and party hard. I found that when I drank alcohol, I could feel my body. A Friday night out would unleash me from my week of mind-focused anxiety and stress. I would lose the frantic feeling lying just beneath my skin, stop the constant rushing, and it soothed me.

I seemed to feel more alive when running on adrenaline so would usually arrive anywhere with only seconds to spare. I was even late for my grandmother's funeral, stopping to breastfeed my baby outside the front of the church. I was always running from one event to the next, not really noticing the present moment, except for when I had some alcohol on board. Then I could laugh and relax.

It felt good to me, normal to be that busy rushing around. Everyone else seemed to be doing it too. What was going on inside my body though was not good. The adrenaline shooting through every cell was shouting "danger," which meant that my body responded by diverting most of its energy away from my immune system and into fight or flight or "possum in the headlights," my usual stress response.

My heart was always racing, my leg muscles constantly tensed to run. When the deep upper leg muscles, the psoas, that run from belly to thigh are engaged for action, they impact the gut, where 80 percent of our serotonin, our feel-good chemical, is first made. Living in fight or flight day to day, as so many of us live, also screws with your head— diverting blood flow away from your smart front brain and into your simple hindbrain, your cavewoman brain. It makes sense to have a simple brain so you can make simple "run, fight, hide" decisions that could save your life. But the problem was that I was living this way full-time and couldn't use the imaginative, loving, feeling, connective, empathetic, joyful, and passionate parts of myself—too busy on the mouse wheel of stress.

Our world is in the middle of a stress pandemic. It is thought that more than 80 percent of current doctor and hospital visits are due to living stressed-out lives. Stress screws with your mind and your body, and most of us don't have a clue what that does to our insides.

Another stress chemical causing mayhem in my body at that time was something called cortisol. Cortisol is a very smart chemical with an ancient knowing; it goes off human stress history and tells your body that with this much stress going on, there must be some serious danger around you, so "Prepare for war! Watch out for famine and don't get pregnant—it's not safe!" Cortisol tells your body to either eat everything in sight and store it on belly, bum, and hips, or don't feel hungry, don't feel anything. It tells your adrenal glands to stop making progesterone, a key antianxiety and fertility hormone for women. For me, it meant that I either missed periods or had heavy, painful periods, and when I threw in a Friday night of alcohol, my liver could not get rid of the excess estrogen and sent it to store as a dodgy form of estrogen in my cervix, belly, and breasts.

We are not meant to have difficult periods or difficulty in conceiving. It is just not that complicated—cut stress, and your body can make the hormones it needs to keep your body calm, peaceful, and able to do what it does best. But almost everyone around you is too busy rushing around, and this does some crazy stuff to your internal chemistry.

Stress starves the immune system of power so it is unable to grab and remove misbehaving cells. It can't do its job. Shortly after leaving my husband, I was diagnosed with pre-cancer of the cervix and had it removed, but I did not wake up to why it was there in the first place. No one told me what stress could do to your hormones and to your health, and I didn't think to ask. I just kept on with my mad constant rushing through my days.

SCARS ON THE BODY

I met Will when I was thirty-three years old, and he turned my world upside down. A positive interrupt to my solitary, mind-based way of living. A great soul smash happened that has caused me the most pain and yet has been one of the most powerful connections of my life.

We met in a bar aptly named the Soul Bar, but that was not the first time I had seen him. When I was sixteen, I had sneaked into a nightclub with my sister and saw him there in the middle of a group on the dance floor. He had come to the city from his hometown three hours away for a running tournament. I can still see him clearly on that dance floor laughing with his friends. I watched him from a balcony above and felt deeply drawn to him but was not brave enough to move, to go and talk to him before friends dragged me out of the club and away into the night.

Within a few months of meeting Will, he asked me to marry him, and I kept saying I was not ready. After a difficult divorce, I was nervous about walking into another marriage. I felt that it would trap me and engulf my freedom and my peace that I had so worked hard to gain. I was not sure of him; he was not like anyone I had ever met before, and my ego that desired the fairy-tale man struggled. He was not a university-educated person that I could challenge to an ego duel. He did not do mind games but led from the heart and was incredibly intuitive. He was in a business where he counseled and helped businesses and business owners heal, and I could tell by the way his clients loved him that he was healing so much more than their bottom-line profitability.

I could not make sense of this man. None of my hiding worked with him. He seemed too good as a person. He wasn't able to judge others, and this scared my mind and untrusting body as he relentlessly delved deep into finding "me," who I was under my stories and well-constructed critical armor. So many nights he would not let me escape into sleep or silence as he questioned and opened my scarred, hidden self, a self that not even I had faced, and he would talk with me until the story, the fear, was completely cleaned out, often until the birds came up at dawn.

I could feel myself unpeel layers of old overcoats that I had used to cover my soul. Some of them would come away with ease and a rush of freedom and delight, but others would rip from my very soul with so much discomfort it felt like my skin went with it. Will's constant gentle questioning rattled me into a knowing of truth about myself and made my mind and body open into another way to be. And still, I resisted him, my mind desperate to remain in charge, my ego wanting separation, a reason to disconnect, escape from deeper knowing. Not sure of him, of trusting men.

One weekend, Will took me to a fancy restaurant for dinner, and the Italian opera singer wandering around the restaurant sang my grandfather's favorite song—a song so special to me, as my grandfather was a beautiful, loving man who sang opera like heaven. At the end of the beautiful aria, in front of the restaurant, Will dropped to his knees and laid a ring on my finger. I could not resist anymore; I said yes. Something in me knew this challenging journey was good for me. He would not let me stand still, hide out in my own world, and although it was painful to drop my fears, to walk with him, I knew I had to keep going—find more, open more.

The rebellion in my body and mind to releasing the ego showed itself just before our wedding ceremony. I got the final wake-up call to stop leading by my reptilian mind—to step up and find my full heart. A few weeks before, as we had lain together in bed, Will noticed a tiny pea-sized lump in my breast, and I went through a ridiculous amount of scans, X-rays, and other biopsies. I was told that I had breast cancer, but I believed that I could have that removed and get on with my life, like so many other women.

That day, only four days out from our wedding, I was going to get the results from my specialist from further testing. When I found that the final X-rays hadn't come back yet, I didn't hesitate to drive up the road to the lab and collect them myself.

Appearances indicate metastatic disease to the mid and lower lumbar spine.

Reading the results in the radiology car park stopped time for me. The madness stopped. The results said that I had secondary cancer in the spine. I knew what that meant, and these words played in my head:

Breast cancer gone wild.
Spread through the body.
Only a few months to live …

Two hours later, I was lying inside an MRI scanner, feeling embarrassed and upset. My specialist was desperate to see if there was anything else they could do for me and had pulled some strings to get me this urgent scan. I had run out of the house that hot summer's morning with just a tight sundress on and no underwear. I was now feeling the cold steel of the scanner beneath my butt in a backless hospital gown. I was freezing and uncomfortable with needles in both arms. Suddenly, I felt the most indescribable rage pour through my heart, hot all over with it. I was angry. Angry at God.

I had let go of religion by that time of my life. As I entered my late teens, the disconnection between human imperfection, guilt, and religion was too much for me to make sense of, so I had sent spirituality into the too-hard basket and saw all those who had faith as utterly naive.

Now, though, in that coffin-like space, I yelled out to the great Universal Force. It was all I had left to do.

If anyone is there, I am so pissed at you. What the hell? I have a little six-year-old girl who is going to be left alone. I'm getting married in a few days. What have I done that is so bad that I deserve this?

It felt good to say it, and then I got an answer. A big one.

Suddenly I felt deliciously warm all over. I felt a blanket of light, of warmth, above me in the scanner, and I heard these words, said playfully with a sense of humor: "Isn't this what you wanted? A dramatic ending? The Katherine Mansfield ending, pale and interesting, with all your family around you saying good-bye?"

I knew this to be true. At university, I loved reading about Katherine Mansfield, a writer who left New Zealand in the 1920s and lived a richly bohemian life where she enjoyed male and female lovers. She married a very controlling man and lived in France with him but felt suffocated by his energy and died young, the same age I was now, of tuberculosis. I knew in every part of my being that I was choosing my death. Something in me wanted it. To fly away finally from this body I had so much discomfort being in. To find another way to be that was more real, freer.

I lay there for a few moments soaking that in. Feeling the warmth of the huge light energy wrapping around me, a sense of its patient love, sense of humor, and deep acceptance of my predicament. I felt a question rise in me, and I called out to the warmth wrapping me in the cold belly of the scanner.

So … I choose. And if I get to choose, what if I choose something else?

Immediately a plethora of images, a Technicolor movie began to play in front of my eyes. I saw my hand in my daughter's, her hand all grown up, wearing a beautiful gown, walking her down the aisle. I saw myself laying in a hospital bed with bandages on my chest but knowing deep in my heart that after that I would be healthy, that I would not need any further medical care. I saw an image of my hands, with golden light pouring out of them, and then image after image of sitting with others, hearing them, a hand on them as they calmed, watching people ignite into health, away from fear, sadness, or despair. I saw my belly round with a child, holding babies and on stage teaching, guiding others to be peaceful and heal their bodies. I saw a pile of books to be created. I saw much laughter, passion, swimming naked, extraordinary living.

This amount of full-on living scared me. I had never experienced life like this. I had lived much more carefully and critically. I could see that if I took this option I had been shown, I would be leaving behind a normal life. I would be different, and life would be way outside the picket fence I had valued so highly.

In that moment, I knew that I had been so unhappy trying to fit into a normal life. The ache within me could not be filled with a perfect wedding, perfect marriage, job, party, or shopping; none of those things could ever fill me. That life was not a life that held me anymore. A life was to be who you really were.

So I lay there with the seesaw of choice in front of me. Death felt like an easier option, no risk of humiliation in that. Or I could live a big, strange but powerfully free and authentic-to-me life helping others. I wavered for a moment and then felt a deep call within, a desire to live and live another way.

Go on then. Let's do this. I'll stay. I choose to stay.

At that moment, the power surged in the scanner; I felt my body undulate with electricity head to toe. Only recently I was reading some new scientific research into the way cancer cells work. Faulty electrical signaling between cells and the spaces between cells can grow cancer. I was being given a universal reboot of sorts—an electrical one, a thrum, and a sound that I could feel deep into my genetic coding. I watched as the scared, small me, the fearful one, sat up and walked out of my body and out of the scanner into ether. I felt great warmth and a lighter energy, an improved version of me, land inside my skin, making my whole body feel long, heavy, and powerful. The speaker in the MRI crackled as the radiographer told me that they needed to reboot the scanner and to keep very still. They were going to redo my scans.

Forty-five minutes later, a different woman left the hospital than the one who had gone in.

A few hours later, I met with the oncologist. He had assessed my MRI scans and had talked them through with several colleagues in New Zealand and overseas. Although he could not explain why the earlier X-rays and scans had shown the cancer had spread into my spine, he smiled and said, "I have an early wedding gift for you. The new MRI scans show no cancer there."

His thought was that the X-rays and other tests must have just been very sensitive to picking up some old injury in my lumbar spine. I had been in a car accident several years before that had written off my car, but I had walked out of it with a sprained wrist, that was all. No back pain. But I was happy to hear his explanation of the sudden test changes. I did not delve deeper or try to explain what I had experienced in the scanner. I felt as though I had almost dreamed it, and so I picked the little Indian oncologist up and hugged him with all my strength, dancing the poor guy around the room.

Calling my family and friends that evening to tell them that the doctors said that they could now operate on me was amazing. Isn't it funny how life gets into perspective when you are told you don't have any options and then find that you do? My parents were so excited that I could now have surgery that they sat outside and toasted my health with champagne under the night stars.

So I was booked for having my breast tissue beneath the skin and nipple removed from my right breast and an implant put in its place. One way of getting a boob job! I knew deep in my heart that after surgery I would be well and 100 percent healthy, even if most people around me were unsure.

I did not know how to make sense of what I had experienced in that machine. I did not feel that I could share it with anyone, and I did wonder if I had dreamed it. I was left with a deep knowing that I would be okay, that cancer was not going to kill me. The anxiety had dulled, and a sense of humor and calm had landed within. A knowing that I was here for something greater than myself was present now.

Will seemed to understand this just as clearly too. He became fearless and argued intensely with the hospital the night before surgery to stop them from cutting out all my lymph nodes in my armpit along with my breast. They were determined that cancer had to be in my lymph glands from the test results and the spread of cancer through the breast. He told them point-blank that I was refusing to have my nodes removed, that I would agree to have surgery the next day only if someone from the lab would be there who would look at my first node under the microscope and check it for cancer. I would agree to have all my nodes taken only if there was proven cancer there.

I am sure they thought I was wasting all their time; they had not seen someone with my test results without a spread into the nodes. Will stood in my corner. At ten o'clock the night before surgery, we had an agreement to have someone who would come in from the lab.

When my first node came out, the lab technologist checked it under the microscope and saw no cancer outside the breast area. My breast was removed from under my skin, a wonderfully kind plastic surgeon then inserted a new breast implant, and that was me, done and dusted, finished with cancer and with any further cancer treatment.

When I was recovering in the hospital, I felt a warm energy that would come and go. It felt like someone was sitting next to me. I could feel the weight of a small body sending waves of soothing, warm light toward me. It didn't bother me at all. I knew whatever was sitting next to me was very healing. My sister came and visited me one morning, and I felt the weight next to me on the bed again. She turned white; she could sense it too. I told her not to be concerned; whoever was there with us was bringing only love.

SCARS OF A MIRACLE

Six weeks later, recovered and settling in back at home, I got some extraordinary news. When my period did not come that first month after surgery, I was not concerned, as I thought the impact of surgery must have shocked my system and it was still recovering. Only ten days post surgery, I had finished with all medication and was on the road to full healing.

My body was not still in recovery, I was pregnant. The night Isabella was conceived, William had seen a vision of a great meteor shooting across the sky. He turned to me and said, "Honey, I am pretty sure you're pregnant, and this kid is a powerful being." He has done this with both our children—known immediately when their spirit arrived.

I had thought at the time how beautiful that would be but was not sure my body was ready after everything it had just gone through.

Getting pregnant this quickly after cancer surgery shocked a lot of people—doctors, family, and friends. I was lucky to meet a surgeon who was not afraid to speak it as he saw it. He told me that although getting pregnant when you had breast cancer could increase the speed of the cancer growth, they really didn't know much about how people got on getting pregnant only a few weeks after surgery. He smiled at me and said, "Sounds like a good reason to just be happy. Why don't you go and enjoy your baby!"

I couldn't stop smiling after that. It seemed like a beautiful fresh start, although most people thought we were completely mad. When I told people that I was pregnant, I got a lot of wince-filled half smiles. I could see that they thought I was most likely bringing into the world a child who would soon be motherless.

The fear people hold toward cancer when you are young is extraordinary. How friends behave is interesting. The ones you think will be there for you usually are. Family can become a loving extension of your healing, but there are some who just can't handle being around you. Their own fear of death takes them over; either they have lost someone close to them or they have a deep subconscious fear that they might catch it. Ironically, one of the most amazing souls to turn up and hold space for me with all her warmth, had lost her own darling mum to breast cancer. Briar's grief scar had made her heart so full with love.

When Isabella arrived, I breastfed off one breast, and my body seemed to know how to make enough milk to cover all her needs. It was funny watching the transition of my breasts over this time. A breast-feeding breast can get pretty enormous! So I had to use a chicken fillet-like plastic insert in my bra over my mastectomy boob when going out to get a matching pair.

One morning when Isabella was a couple of months old, I was invited to have morning tea with a friend. Instead of meeting at her place, she had asked if I would meet her at the local hospital café, as she was visiting someone there. I was triggered and itchy about meeting up at the same hospital where I had my breast surgery, but I went anyway.

Halfway through the catch-up, I realized with a start that it was exactly one year to the day since my surgery, and I took my wee babe upstairs to the ward to see the nurses who had taken such loving care of me. It felt so good to go up to that ward, healthy with my child in my arms, taking new life into a place where so many women were in fear of their own. I felt such warmth seeing the nurses holding Isabella in their arms, beaming with happiness.

Around this time, the singer Kylie Minogue was diagnosed with breast cancer. Outside the local shop, I saw a women's magazine headline saying something negative about her ability to have children. I was furious and rang the editor. They published an article with me shortly after with the just as unappealing byline "Cancer Mum Gives Kylie Hope." I am not a cancer mum; I am a healthy mum. Before Isabella was born, I appeared in another magazine with my pregnant belly to show others how beautiful life can be after cancer; again though, the article was heavily influenced into fear mongering around breast cancer.

The week after I stopped breast-feeding Isabella, I was pregnant once again with Liam, a son after three girls for our family. William had a vision of a dark, curly-haired boy who would come into our life; he got it right again. The universe had given me a long healing hormone treatment with the two pregnancies and breast-feeding that allowed my body to heal beautifully. When I finished breast-feeding, I had a new nipple tattoo created over my mastectomy breast and an implant placed in my now tiny left breast to even them out. I had been naming them Perky and Floppy, so with help from a plastic surgeon who was also very intuitive and respectful of my journey, I felt pretty wonderful.

When Isabella was old enough to speak sentences, she told me that she remembered "the time before she chose me and Daddy." She told us that she used to come and visit me when I was sick and in the hospital. She also described how she had seen my mother crying while standing in our kitchen preparing meals for us all when I was recovering at home. She spoke of how she had tried to send her love to tell her all would be okay. Isabella described the house in detail although we had moved from there by the time she was born. She said she had chosen to come and help me "heal my insides."

———

Life went back to normal family life but not the old normal. I couldn't *do* negativity anymore. It seemed silly and dramatic. I felt every moment, every emotion. I felt hungry and could actually taste food. I felt saucy and passionate. I found I could not listen to critical language or critical people, watch aggressive movies, see television advertising, or hear angry music. I found myself stopping in the day, tears in my eyes as I saw a bee on a leaf or a child's smile. I had changed.

My hands would turn hot when I was near someone who was not in a good way. I would look at them, and although I had no idea why, I could see areas of grayness on their body where something was wrong physically, mentally, or emotionally. As I focused on someone, medical terminology would land in my mind. I would hear words like "bicuspid valve" or "anterior cruciate ligament." My physiology and anatomy skills were not the best then, but somehow I was being given a clear vision of exactly the part of a person's body that was looking for transformation—even at times right down deep inside cells or genetic coding.

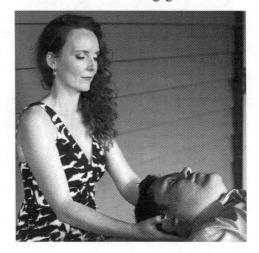

As I placed my hand gently on the area concerned or focused on it, I would watch the grayness break away like fine ash, and people could feel the heat in my hands and inside their own body as it began to heal itself inside out.

SCARRED TO HEAL

My work heals me, and every day I learn something more about myself as I help others. I see my service as supporting people to awaken into their own beauty, health, and joy and to better understand their own gift of service to this planet.

I have the ability to hear and translate what the body requires to be freer energetically when I work with others. The body always knows what the priority is. Often it is around clearing emotional junk that feels to me like a layer of sludge in the cells. When you attune telepathically, the person or animal will tell you exactly what is holding them back at that moment.

Although I gather my client's personal body and medical story when I work with them, I am more interested in what I sense, feel, and hear that is not being said. Often the traumatic life stories we attach to can stop the body from finding greater health and well-being. The quiet conversation I can hear from the heart and body tells so much more than the story filtered by the mind.

When I tune into someone, what is going on physically usually comes second to the emotional story from the body. The emotional energy has usually created the physical discomforts in the body, so it makes sense to clear that up first. Some of the early emotional events that happen to us leave great marks in the body, even though in mind and heart we may feel we have moved on.

When the body can release this held energy, there is more vitality and joy available. In placing my hands on someone, I hear the emotion that is the problem, such as "abandonment," "hate," "resentment," or "powerlessness" and then the who or why it was there in the first place. Often I am shown a vision of the moment in time when it arrived in the body. The body is simply asking for resolution of the feeling so it can use more of its power for creating a happier and healthier life experience.

One law I have learned that is deeply sacred in this universe of ours is *free will*. You cannot interfere with that. I always check in and ask permission before engaging with someone's pain or disease. I cannot offer help if someone does not want to heal or release what is causing the pain. They have to give me permission to connect with their field of energy and their internal world. This is sometimes frustrating for clients who want me to work on a family member or a friend who is struggling. When I connect with someone who doesn't want to shift from the pain they are in, I feel and hear a clear "No!" I can hear it as clearly as if they were yelling it right at me. I always respect that and leave them be. If they want help, they will find me or someone else at a time that suits them, or not, and that's just fine. I work with people all over the world for healing. It doesn't matter if someone is next to me or on the other side of the world, I can feel how he or she is doing.

When I first began exploring this healing gift, I would mirror other people's aches and pains in my own body, and when I felt their discomfort or pain release, I would feel it rocking energetically down my own spine and away. This was hard, confusing, and physically exhausting, and I realized I couldn't keep doing this. When meditating into why my body was mirroring this way, I saw that many of us carry stuck or painful experiences as memory in the body. When the body releases this energetically, it is a blast through the major energy centers of the body from crown through to feet. I often see a great light from above the head washing down the center of the body, at the same time I see a great light from the heart of the earth roar up through their feet. This ignition of universal and earth—a balance of male and female energy—offers a great cleanup, allowing room for more health and new vitality.

In becoming more aware of spiritual ego and releasing any need to feel that I was part of the healing process, I shifted my intention to becoming more of an observer to healing, and that calmed the physical mirroring down by about 80 percent. It became much easier to continue doing the work. I have learned to get out of the way and be more neutral.

I often wake in the early hours with answers to issues I am facing, or with people in mind to send healing to, and over the last decade I have been given a healing manual of sorts in these early morning downloads. I know that my job is pretty simple. I show people the road where they can let go of old stories so they can access their own way back to health if they choose it. I no longer attach to a need for them to choose it or not. We live thousands of lives, and it is not my place to decide if one life is better than another, or should be expressed in a certain manner, healthy or not. Working this way stops my ego, mind, and body from attaching to another person's healing or intervening for a particular outcome that is none of my business. Where this is hard is when I become very close to someone. There is always that very real human desire to help them heal—to see them become their most powerful self.

Offering healing is simply to *be* a wide vibration of health and observe the person orienting to that energy in their own timing. The key is not to push too much too fast. It often takes decades to lay down the layers of fears and anxieties that have led to the mental or physical conditions that we have, and the best way to release them is gently at a pace that is comfortable. That is why many clients work with me a handful of times, weekly or monthly, and heal themselves slowly and surely. With babies, it usually only takes moments for them to release and unwind held tension and stress or birth trauma, as they do not have the layers of fear identities holding them down. In the case of cancer, I have often seen immediate release, as I had. It is always amazing to witness the miraculous lift of gray cancer energy and watch as the body chooses to ignite the immune system and flush health through organs and tissues. Body transformation is a beautiful thing.

After having faced death and working with many people who are dying, death is not something to be afraid of. It is something we all experience. For some of us, we choose disease as a wake-up call into a more authentic way of living, or to serve a greater subconscious purpose/audience that can learn from our experience. For some though, they are either overwhelmed by fear energy or they have simply completed their journey in this form and desire to go home to All That Is. That is okay too. I have often felt these words pouring from the bodies of those who are choosing to leave this world early: "I have done what I came here to do, and I don't have a purpose now to stay."

If they come to my clinic, often a purpose—a new one—does turn up to be offered. I do have an intention in my clinic, that if you come to me, you are seeking a cleanup of sorts or you are looking for *another way to be* from what you are currently experiencing. It is lovely to see someone who feels that there is no hope lift their head to possibility and potential. I have seen many miraculous shifts in people who have decided to try opening another door to a chance at this life. My job is not to keep people alive though if they don't want to stay.

Working with the dying is a beautiful opportunity to see the beauty of who we are, and often all people are looking for at the end of life is a gentle release of all of the held pain from a life well lived—to forgive those who need to be released from them, to love those who have filled them with joy, so they can release lightly from this realm.

It is not always easy to be the way I am. As my intention is to clear away the debris people carry around their natural light, my energy can be confronting for those who identify with fear. I have had many instances where I am seated on a plane next to someone, at the movies, or another event where the person next to me gets very uncomfortable, wriggles around, and then finds an excuse to move elsewhere. I have people cross the street as I walk by. I am smiling writing this from a sun lounger in Fiji. I have only been seated for a few minutes, but the couple next to me just packed up and moved to another part of the pool. It used to hurt, watching people run, but not anymore. Now, I just smile and know that my energy pours a light where it will.

Fear fights for survival, and often a person's identity is heavily attached to it—to the world being a crappy place. If they see themselves as a victim, or angry and distrustful toward others, unconditional love energy turning up next to them will feel very itchy and uncomfortable. Even friends, people I love can sometimes get upset with me seeing things they are not yet ready to see or seeing too much and not giving them privacy to have hidden parts of themselves. Those of us who are here to wake people up are meant to be an annoying interrupt!

People often ask what I see when I work with them. I usually work with my eyes closed with my hand laid softly over their heart or cradling their head as they lay down. Behind my eyelids, I see visions of why their pain is there. I often see moments of trauma; I see them as a baby or child, accidents, rape, arguments, or other life events that have left a scar in the body. The body remembers all the events and doesn't have a sense of time so will hold onto the energy of trauma until it is released energetically or physically. That is why I see so many people who have had years of counseling therapy unable to find full release until we work together with their body. They are often amazed how free they can feel when that ball of old energy is expelled.

Our minds love to store and rehash the difficult stories like a library of self. My job is to help those I work with realize that they are a body, heart, and mind, and change means taking the claws off the past and releasing the old, letting it go for good.

Forgiving those who have caused you great pain is vital, as rage and resentment cause a chemical soup of grayness in the body. Unhooking from those who have harmed you creates space. For the body to use all its systems as it should for healing, for being present to life, rather than focusing on old past pain.

All my senses are involved in this work. Sometimes it is a clear vision, words, or conversation from the body around what needs to go, and sometimes I can smell the burning rubber from a car accident or the smell of terror. I have learned to observe from a wide, tall space and not get lost in what I see, feel, and hear. It always comes back to this gentle question: is there another way to be?

I learned to ask this question and how to become wider and more neutral from a dear soul brother who turned up in my life at just the right time. I met Frédéric at a party not long after I began taking clients and could feel his healer energy immediately. He taught me a modality called craniosacral therapy. It is around feeling the breath of life as it travels down the spine and out into the nervous system, of also being a respectful, wide container of neutrality and using gentle touch to offer shift and change in health without expecting an outcome. Studying this work and bringing it into my practice gave me the ability to keep going without burning out. It meant that I could become more like that energy that held me in the MRI scanner, a graceful presence without being overwhelmed by a client's pain or trauma.

People have many reactions when I work with them. Many lay back on the treatment table and fall asleep immediately so their minds can check out and their bodies can more easily get on with healing. Some can get quite emotional as they feel the layers of old fear and pain leave them. I have even had some experience full-body sweats before crossing the threshold to the room as the fear makes a last-ditch effort to stay present. My intention is always to create a gentle space of compassion where there is no right or wrong, where they can feel heard and held safely, a sacred space where they can be profoundly vulnerable and know they have arms to catch them.

Although I might have a huge ex-army tattooed man on my table, I can feel the tender and fragile child self under the layers of serious adult concrete overcoats. Working from a wide space of unconditional care, I feel under my fingers the body tense and then profoundly release the story, the trauma, the old un-forgiveness, disease, hatred, or pain. It simply melts off them like water and out the door. I have watched people who have taken another person's life forgive themselves, and I have seen the spirit of the person they have killed leave their field of energy and walk away in peace. It is wonderful to see how beautiful we are as human beings, how gentle we each are under the surface of well-trained fear and control. Each of us is unique, a great treasure, a sacred jigsaw piece in this great world puzzle, and I know something for certain—there is no such thing as normal or perfect.

I do not work on my own. I always feel a great circle of light beings—angels—working with me. I am just one of a team holding space for the client on the table. Sometimes I am told to step back and get out of the way if the energy with that person is particularly fierce, such as murder or deep violence. I feel Archangel Michael gently removing my hand and standing in front of me, taking over.

I remember working with a man who had been in jail, and when I began to see and feel the terrible abuse he had suffered as a child start to pour out of his belly as he lay snoring on the treatment table, my chair with me on it got picked up and wheeled to the other side of the room. I watched as Archangel Michael reached into the man's belly and pulled out an angry-looking Maori *taniwha*. (Maori water monster). Then, gently, my chair was pushed back to the table and my hand led to pour a new calm compassion into his belly. I often see client's eyes change color after these sessions. I do not share what I have seen. It serves no purpose. They feel free, beautiful, and new. When the old pain is gone, it's gone.

Most people would get very angry if you suggested that we choose disease or illness, especially if they are a parent of a child experiencing a life-threatening or debilitating condition that is causing the whole family so much pain. I would never say anything about subconscious creation of health or disease to a parent or to someone suffering, although when I have worked with a sick child, I can feel why they are choosing to have that disease or experience and who will receive the learning as a result. We have many hundreds or thousands of lives on this planet, and they are like a video game where sometimes we play a role to serve others. At a deep subconscious level, we understand that we are all integrally connected, and by one person learning, we all learn.

What I do know is that people's choices are much more complicated than we realize; often at a subconscious level the experience they are choosing affects a great ring of other people. Deep within us there is an understanding that in this short life, each of our experiences impact others.

HELP FROM ANGELS

I have learned to trust the conversation I continue to experience with the universe, and it feels beautifully comforting to know that this great warm presence guides me each unique day, guides us all and has our back. I see signs of this vast energy everywhere. I go into a bookshop, and a book often falls off the shelves in front of me, giving me tools on different healing modalities or, as the universe would have it, a nudge about something I need to release in my own life.

I often find white feathers in strange places—on the seat of my car, under the bed, in my handbag. Often I find them when I am having a challenging moment—a tough client, a problem with a relationship, with the kids, when I am feeling down. Finding these feathers always makes me smile and stops my groaning. I realize that I am never alone; I am part of a nonvisible but present healing tribe, and that's good.

When I first began my tiny clinic, I did not completely trust myself. I felt that I could help the few people that would come to me, but outside the room, I tried to be "normal" like everyone else and not say too much about these new feelings and gifts that had arrived. It is often like this for intuitive people; we don't want to be ridiculed or humiliated.

One afternoon in those early days, I went down to the local organic store for some groceries. As I walked in, the place felt different, like time had slowed. As I rounded the aisles, I noticed that no one was there, and then I saw him. A very tall man with shoulder-length dark curls wearing the store's green apron. He came smiling around the corner and up to me. He looked at me, and I caught my breath. He was indescribably bright, too beautiful to meet eye to eye. He looked at me and with a cheeky smile said, "You are a healer, aren't you?"

I didn't know what to say. I just stared at him and said, "No, not really. But I have a room, and I'm learning."

He cocked his head on one side and looked at me intently. "I have a problem with my shoulder. Can you place your hands on it for me?"

I froze.

"Look, I would have to see you in my room to do that." I had turned beet red and was very uncomfortable. He smiled and reached out for my hand.

"No you don't. You don't need a room when you have those hands with you all the time, Veronica."

Before I could think any further, about how he knew my name, I reached up to his enormous shoulder and placed my hand on him, closing my eyes. Great radiating lights exploded behind my eyelids, and I felt a shooting heat under my finger, and then I shakily let go. Standing there, still amazed, I felt him move off around another aisle, and the moment was gone. I could hear and feel a change in the atmosphere around me. Suddenly there were people jostling past, wheeling shopping carts and chatting at the checkout desk. I shook my head and picked up my basket and went to pay.

Still feeling stunned by what had happened, I asked the young woman serving me who the tall, young man was that worked there. She smiled at me, confused, and said that she was the only one working there that afternoon.

I knew I had met an angel that day, and I stopped doubting my gift and trying to make mental sense of it. I realized that I get to see what I now call "the Back Room," a dimensional shift between time where you can witness the reasons for current troubles. Sometimes this will take me to seeing things back in a person's lifetime, or to their future, sometimes into different realms entirely. I have lost count of how many times I have had to reach into a man's body and pull out a sword or an arrow from an ancient wound, not from this life.

It makes sense when we realize that we are a soup of thousands of generations. We do not just carry our ancestor's gene for blue eyes or artistic gift but also some of their past traumas, anxieties, fears, and despair. Sometimes I get to see whole movies of experiences while my hands are resting on a person's body. I do not enter into conversation with what I see, make it right or wrong; I just keep with the program and ask "if there is another way it could be" and see the battle, war cries, barbed wire, and mud disappear. I feel the body under my fingers drop into peace, all while the person is asleep. I rarely share what I see, as it would be too confusing or confronting. Many of the visions are outside the realm of imagination or even words!

After meeting the angel, I began to deeply trust the message I had been given of being available wherever required and no longer let my head get in the way. I have a lot of lost kids come to me in public places and being able to soothe and calm them before reuniting them with their parents is great, but often the gift is more powerful than that. These young ones are here to make the world better than how it is, and a moment of pure presence with them helps them remember why they are here and not to get lost in fear. Appropriate societal behavior leaves the building when in the depths of this work as you give the person you are with what they need, the words they need to hear right then for healing.

I have helped several people recover in the midst of a heart attack or stroke. One day I was sharing a birthday lunch with my mother and my sister in a café when I noticed a man in his late forties walk past the sidewalk in front of the window and grab at his arm. His face turned gray and he stopped mid-stride. Immediately I got up, ran to him, and told him to look at me. Our eyes locked as I placed my hand over his heart and felt it beat strongly once more. The color returned to his face. I then went back inside and quickly sat down. The man walked into the café, looked at me strangely for a moment, shook his head, and went and ordered a coffee. My mother and sister just continued their conversation. I have had so many moments like that, where time slows and people don't really see what is going on around them. It is very cool to be able to jump into the Back Room and give people that healing gift.

It is not easy sometimes to hold space for people when they are in pain. Sometimes their reflection, their scars remind me of my own, of feelings and fears that I am yet to let go of myself. Often we are trying to reconcile old pain stories from earlier on in life, maybe a difficult parent who had trouble showing emotion or one that showed too much, so we seek out the same person in a cascade of different bodies to play out the drama over and over again. After a while though, you tire of experiencing the same game, and I find it helpful to ask clients I work with the hard question: "What is the payoff for continuing this pattern?"

When you can get to that and let go of the dopamine chemical rush of rejection, abandonment, humiliation, or those other feelings we are often drawn to reconcile, they go, and you are left with more space within to create a newer and happier version of you.

As I continue to explore my gift that began in the MRI scanner, I notice that what I can feel is the great soup of energy that we are all connected to. I am not anything special. We all have the ability to tune into it if we choose to. This is why we could be doing the dishes at the sink with our back turned and be able to feel if our partner's energy is happy or angry when they walk in behind us. It is also why we get a sense about a person when we first meet them. I remember reading somewhere that more than 70 percent of us have experienced thinking about someone and then getting a call or message from them. There is nothing spooky about this; this is just a field of energy we all share, and it is useful to be aware of it and pour warmth into it.

This field of energy is what advertising companies use to coerce us to buy products or shift behavior. They understand that if they get a great enough number of people focused, then the energy flows out into the grid around to everyone else, and what they are selling becomes universally acceptable. Ever wondered why suddenly all young men are wearing the same hairstyle and beard? Why suddenly everyone thinks getting married makes you a "bridezilla," or suddenly every food is salted caramel flavor? The field of energy is understood and manipulated by not all good sources. I like to think there are enough of us beings of light putting light into the field to support some balance.

This great universal field of energy is shared among all living things. Animals work off that field of energy better than humans, and so this deep listening-healing and telepathic connection works very well for them. Although I don't focus on animal work these days, most days one of the neighboring animals and local birds turn up at my healing clinic Angels Rest if they need healing or support. I have a black Labrador that visits from several houses away from time to time telling me of how his "parents" won't stop fighting and can I do something about it. I have a regular kookaburra that brought his wounded friend with a cracked beak yesterday. Life is certainly much more interesting than before I got sick.

There have been many miraculous stories. I have worked with several young women with breast cancer over the years, and I wouldn't have earned the right to do it without experiencing my own health scars. It is incredible to see a fearful body drop into deep, wide relaxation and turn the immune system back up to full power or see people who have had so much trouble with their hormonal health able to access fertility once again because their bodies remember how to drop damaging stress.

Recently my practice has called in children and teenagers who are outside the normal. These kids I call HEBs (highly evolved beings) come with a stressed parent wishing their child could just be more normal. These kids struggle at school and with sleeping, eating, and social connections. Many have been diagnosed with some sort of spectrum disorder. Their parents find it hard and don't know how to help their child fit in. They ask why can't they just eat "normal" food, be more normal?

At this point, I usually ask Mum and Dad to relax outside with a book while I give their child my full attention. HEBs are evolved humans. As evolved humans, their bodies do not want to eat fake food-like items manufactured by people in white coats and loaded with colors, chemicals, and other dangerous nonfood items masquerading as food or beverages. These "normal" foods make them sick, shaky, and angry.

HEBs require food fuelled with sunlight and fresh air and the power of the sea—green leafy vegetables, more of a Japanese diet of sea vegetables, miso soup, and broths. Our planet is not in a good way. Breeding more kids to become accountants and economists who blindly follow consumerism is not going to heal our forests, clean our oceans, or keep our lions alive in the wild. These kids are the brave fledgling plants growing up through the gray concrete and need to be highly celebrated and loved as they push their way into making us a better race of human

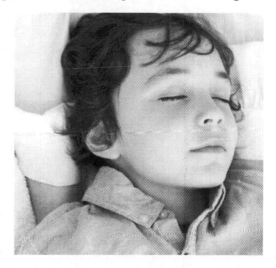

beings. Yes, they are quirky and odd but they are vital for bringing change. They don't care about societal norms, and they aren't meant to. It's the only way they can be brave enough to come up with the innovative global change ideas and healing concepts.

It's really hard raising HEBs. The key as a parent of these children is to find their passion, their pulse, their gift that they came here to offer and do everything you can to find them mentors, support, and help to grow in that space. Forget normal. Forget fitting in. Forget standardized ways of behaving. Just feed them real human food and water, keep them away from poisonous colors, chemicals, flavors, gluten, dairy, and sugar and watch them blossom. They are highly sensitive to stimuli, so watch the amount of digital overload or aggressive information from television or screen-time. Give them lots of hugs and don't worry too much if you wake up and find them snuggled up to you in your bed. The nights are hard for these little guys.

These kids love being in the Back Room space of meditative stillness. They bask in the wide space of unconditional love and remember automatically how to meditate and see deep into their gray matter and remember why they are here. Take them to yoga; take them to a meditation class, as this will feed their soul.

Try not to talk to these kids like they are stupid. They are wise and extraordinarily evolved. Respect them and help them as much as you can. Yes, you are going to require a boatload of patience, but hey, they chose you, so do everything you can to have their backs. Some days it is going to feel like you are not sure how you are going to get through, but you do and you will.

I know, as I have kids just like these myself.

SCARS ON THE HEART

This journey has not been easy. Sometimes I wonder how life would be if I lived it like a "normal" person who had a "normal" marriage, "normal" kids, and spent my days excited about collapsing in front of the TV or buying a new dress at the mall on the weekends. For me, every day I get to explore another part of the journey up the mountainside toward awakening. I get to see where I am not aware, where I am holding too hard, where I am fearful. The universe seems interested in me moving and helping others move as I go.

Living this way has had a dramatic impact on my relationship with Will. We are no longer married but are something more than that. We see each other as sovereign beings that choose to parent together and support each other in our work that helps others. There is nothing left unsaid between us, and at times it has been deeply challenging. We have questioned everything about how we live and the choices we make, and this has led us to question the way we connect with each other on every level.

As we evolved from a married couple into deep spiritual friendship, we began to understand that much of the discomfort and unsaid pain in relationships is between partners who push and pull each other through being too enmeshed. Society teaches couples to hold each other very tightly through ownership and expectation, and it is very hard for people to fulfill those tight roles at times.

I believe that the natural way for humans to live is more like a tribe. For women, I think that to have your children without help from others is very difficult and causes a lot of quiet pain, competitive energy between women, and expectation of perfection within households. So many women I see at Angels Rest struggle with feeling guilty about not being a good enough mother, guilty for wishing they had some time for themselves, guilty for not doing the mothering job "right."

The men I see also struggle. They hide a secret pain of servitude if they are the breadwinners in the family. They feel the pain of a backpack of provision, and they are taught at an early age that this is something not to be spoken of. Most women have no idea that men feel this way. But I see it every day in men with chronic back pain, chest pain, and the desperate desire to escape this constant expectation of provision through alcohol, affairs, or simply dying early.

I know the idea of going back into community living sounds like some sort of hippy commune thinking, but I am not sure if this constant mouse wheel living of a single man and a single woman living in a house and working themselves to the bone to provide everything for their families makes all that many people terribly happy. This stress hurts our bodies, our relationships, and our ability to find happiness. There has to be another way, a simpler way to live in harmony with each other, together and with what our earth offers us. I think more and more people are feeling the call of living a simpler life, growing their own vegetables and sharing resources.

My own life has become more this way, and it has been an unbelievable and hard ride to get here. I had to let go of the Cinderella and the prince relationship model. I had to let go of expecting my partner to provide everything and continue to wear that mantle without complaint. I had to release ownership, and that hurt like hell. I had been pulling away from the conventional idea of how married people behave for a long time, and I know that was very hurtful for Will. I did not like the idea of being owned, of not being able to talk and have deep conversations with other people just because I "belonged" to Will.

Will grew up with a violent mother who walked away when he was a small child. He had learned to fend for himself and bring up his three younger brothers, who still sent him Mother's Day cards. He needed me to not be what his mother was; he needed me to be kind, the cookie-cutter loving wife wearing an apron and smiling while making dinner, and I rebelled from that need, from being that person. Something in me kicked away at it. Although I spent so much of my time being loving and his best friend, I would find myself at parties after a couple of drinks finding someone interesting and begin discussing their life with them. I would get lost in deep, wide conversation and then look over to see Will's face looking at me, wondering why I was repelling him, why I needed that.

I had several soul smashups like this. None of them sexual but intense connections where I fed off a desire to enter mind debate, find out more about myself through those conversations, maybe somehow prove who I was ego to ego and learn about who they were. Part of me was still trying to reconcile the reptile, the mind-based energy I had inside of me and make sense of it. I could not reconcile that energy with my husband. He did not play in that space; instead he tried to help me see and find the fear, the separated thinking behind the need to behave that way.

After one party where I had particularly offended Will with spending all evening talking with some drunk person, I found myself feeling a desperate need to escape, and I ran out the door of our place, through the streets, with Will chasing me and trying to make sense of what I was doing. I began pulling off my clothes, screaming at him, "Take everything, take all of me! What more do you want!"

Bizarrely, no one seemed to hear us. No curtains pulled, and the night was completely still. What I was saying was that I had hit a wall where I couldn't shift any further without it feeling like death. I could not handle the feeling of being owned, by anyone. I was seeking freedom, but from what I didn't know. I felt that I could not evolve any further; my ego did not want to, and I was trying to kick him away. He was so patient with me. We went back to the house and talked until the sun came up, both realizing that we needed to walk with each other and give each other more room to breathe and be who we were without the weight of expectation.

Things began to settle after that, and then we had a hideous life-changing experience that crashed everything apart and turned our roles as partners around. William had been on a spiritual journey exploring his heart and was in an amazing wise space. It was like living with Yoda. All those who knew Will felt that he was someone who had the answers, could solve any problem, and his insight was incredible. Life was good. I was treating many people in my little clinic, and at times Will and I would work together, seeing people free themselves of trauma, sickness, and pain and find a sense of humor, a new way of being, a calmer mind and body.

Then one night, I sat bolt upright at 1:11 a.m. Will was not next to me; he had obviously fallen asleep next to one of the kids while putting them back to bed. Our two little ones are very intuitive and often have intense dreams, so there was usually a walk back and a settling process that often meant one of us would awake in the morning squashed into half a little bed with a small person's arms and legs wrapped around us like a limpet crab.

As I sat up, trying to get my breath back, my heart hammering in fear, I reviewed the multicolored vision I had just had. I knew this was not a dream but a clear forward vision. In my dream, I had been woken up from sleep in the middle of the night, hearing William talking to someone down our long, marbled floor hallway—his voice deathly serious.

"Mate. You don't want to do this. You really don't want to do this. Just leave now and there will be no trouble."

Then I saw him, a strong, powerfully built man backing up into my line of sight through the bedroom door, a knife in his belt right outside my four-year-old son's bedroom. In the vision, I had seen myself leaping out of bed like a screaming banshee and yelling at the guy to "Get the

F out of our house!" This destroyed the calm Will was trying to create and instead fired him into a rage. He shoulder-charged Will, sending him to the ground, and I heard the sickening sound of his head and neck hitting the marble stairs and blood, so much blood pouring from him.

I knew he was gone. Then the man stopped, stared at me, swore at me not to call the police or I would be next, and ran from the place, leaving me kneeling in horror with my dead husband's head in my hands. The children disheveled with bed hair were now awake, crying around me.

So, a hideous vision. I knew it was real. I knew it was coming. I sat up in bed, my heart in my throat, and although I couldn't move, I called out to Archangel Michael.

"Tell me how I can stop this! What can I do? Can I go and lock up every door in the house? Lock the gates? Go find Will and wake him? What?"

My heart felt like it was going to rip out of my chest. In return I heard this: "No, you cannot stop this, but you can change your reaction, and if you want to save Will, you need to do it right now."

"What! What reaction!" I called out in desperation.

"Release all ownership of everything in and of this house. Things are not people. Do it now," Michael said to me clearly.

I sat up and called out to the universe. "Of my own free will, I release all ownership of all possessions, of things, of stuff. I let go. Please, Michael, please, Universe—please help. Hold back violence if this must happen. Please intervene!"

Just like some sort of fairy-tale character, incredibly I fell immediately back into a deep sleep. I woke exactly two hours later hearing the same horrible words from Will's mouth.

"Mate. You don't want to do this. You really don't want to do this. Just leave now and there will be no trouble."

This time as I saw the intruder walk back into my line of sight from our bed, I knew exactly what to do, and as I carefully got up, noticing that my little girl was now asleep next to me, I carefully put on my dressing gown and walked calmly out to meet both men. I put my crossed arms over my chest, one hand flat in front of each shoulder, and stood there looking at him with wide, deep calm, the same calm I use in my treatment sessions. As I stood there, I felt my little girl come join me, her small body next to mine, her arms also crossed, she too in deep, wide calm.

I looked at the man and said, "We don't have any money here, but you can take our watches and our cars. Take what you like, but we have babies here and don't want any trouble. Don't be afraid. Take what you need and then go."

I felt Will behind me. I saw his hands pinned to the sides of his body, unable to speak, unable to move, and I knew Angel Michael was pinning him down—keeping him safe.

The man looked at us and took the watches and the keys and told us he had three more men with weapons outside, and he would hurt us all if we called the police or made any noise. We calmly followed him out to the garage, and we stood in a line watching him as he turned on the car headlights. The intruder did not understand how to start our European car, and Will leaned in to the driver's side and explained what to do to get it going. The car screeched down the driveway, and we saw more heavy-built men come around from the side of our house and race after it. And then they were gone.

Will dropped to his knees and came out of being held down. He was in terror, deep trauma as he rang the police. I could not calm him or calm the children. The police caught the men immediately. We lost nothing that mattered, but William was not the same.

Will is a strong guy with two black belts in martial arts. For him to stand quietly when someone came into his house and threatened his family was emasculating. He was angry, furious at God. I tried to explain that there was something about this connection between him and the intruder, something ancient that needed to be experienced between the two of them—this time without death of either one. I told him that God had stopped death this time. He didn't want to hear it, and he certainly didn't want to hear any more spiritual talk from me.

At a deeper level, Will was furious with me for intervening, for stopping him from trying to protect his family like a man, for not having died trying to get these monsters out. He stopped all connection to his spiritual self, and it was like living with a ghost. He was on edge constantly. He was confused and traumatized.

Our little girl was also deeply traumatized and would not sleep alone. My husband was in horrendous pain, and I did not know what to do. We took our usual annual Christmas holiday with a bunch of friends and their kids by the beach, and it did nothing to bring any peace or happiness to us. Everything we said seemed to trigger each other, and I felt like I was walking on eggshells constantly. Will did not want to talk about the incident, and our little girl was getting more and more fearful, and it was leading us into despair.

I awoke the last day of our beach holiday with another vision. I saw a large white-painted house and beautiful, lush, warm grass.

I heard, "Go to Tauranga. Go. I have a house for you there."

I told Will. His family was from Tauranga, a place nearly three hours down the motorway from where we were currently living. William had ancestral indigenous Māori land from his mother's family there, and he did not want to be reminded of that childhood abusive life again. But I was adamant. The vision was drawing me to find somewhere, anywhere we could create some peace. I said how amazing it would be to find a place of sanctuary, a place to heal. If we moved the children there, Will would still be able to work a few days a week back in Auckland. I was sure this would give him the time he needed away from us to heal. Essentially we were separating in an attempt to heal the both of us and find some peace, but neither of us discussed this.

So we made a detour to Tauranga instead of heading back home to the place that we now did not want to live in, that reminded us of that night that made us all feel so deeply unhappy. I felt excited looking at this small seaside town. It didn't take us long to find the house from the vision. The big white home was built like a castle, strong and radiantly full of light. It had a barn that could be transformed into a healing space and huge organic vegetable gardens and two acres of lush land with beautiful trees. I could feel the joy from the land, the peace of it.

We traveled back home, and I talked to Will about selling our Auckland home. I did not feel safe there anymore. It was too big, too spread out, and we just needed to get out of there. I asked him to do a letting-go exercise with me, and we sat cross-legged on the ground, and we said out loud: "Of our own free will, we release this home. Unhook all our feelings of discomfort or attachment to it and fill it with healing light. Universe, please bring someone, a family to this house who will love it and be happy here."

Exactly three hours later, there was a knock on the front door. A serious man in his forties wearing a smart suit looked at us with big blue eyes. He said that he was not really sure why he was at our doorstep, but his family had missed out on buying a house further down the road, and he had looked at our property on Google maps, and as he was a real estate agent from out of town, he thought he would be cheeky and ask if perhaps there would be any chance we would consider selling up.

Will looked at me gob smacked, and I beamed. I could feel the hand of light on our back, and it only took a short wander around the property for the man to sit down at the dining table with us and make us an offer well in excess of what we had paid, and he told us he wanted to move in as soon as possible.

So, we were free. Free of that house and the memories of it. I pushed Will to buy the home we had seen in Tauranga, and this would mean that he would live away from us four nights a week in Auckland. Part of me believed that having some time apart would heal us all. I knew I did not have the answers for him, and I was growing uneasy living with his trauma around me. William found an apartment on the beautiful Auckland waterfront where he could work and live and then spend weekends with us.

I was happy in my new home, the peace of it. The home looked across a tree-filled valley to the sea beyond and lay on lush gardens and abundant birdlife. I found myself smiling and healed by the sunlight as I pegged washing on the line and felt soft grass beneath my toes and cheeky, fantailed birds danced around my head. The house came with a flagpole, and I had an Angels Rest flag made with great Aslan the lion's face to protect our home. As I looked up the night I sent it up the flagpole, I gasped to see a great cloud angel dancing above me.

The children began to sleep and heal and settled well into country school. I felt safe and warm although I could not ignore the sense of unease and discomfort between William and me. I knew he missed his family, but I could not reach him. I did not know how to heal his deep painful trauma, heal his anger at the universe.

We transformed the barn into a miraculous healing retreat, and people began to come for healing. I could feel great light pouring into the room, into their bodies, minds, and hearts. Miraculous healing began there. When our neighbor was diagnosed with breast cancer, I felt sure our connection was meant to be. She came to the table, and I watched as she released cancer from her body and called in health once again. I saw many families, mothers and children, who had experienced difficult or invasive childbirth find their bond and unwind trauma from bodies. There were so many beautiful moments.

I was peaceful and happy in this small town. I began to gather a soul tribe of friends, artists, musicians, yogis, healers, and gardeners.

Such joyful, loving, and deeply giving spiritual beings—they opened my heart, and I truly felt at home.

When my neighbor began building a real hobbit hole that I could watch from my window, I smiled. I truly felt I was living in Narnia or Middle Earth with such warm and genuine people. I had to find an electrician to set up some lights for my treatment room, and I giggled when a red-haired, plaited and bearded hobbit character called Bren turned up. He told me he had worked on the set of *Lord of the Rings*, and immediately we fell into easy spiritual conversation about ethereal things. This was the way of this place. Such sublime presence—every breath, moment, tree rustle, and deep, eye-crinkling smile was slow and real.

Meanwhile, I knew William was alone and brooding in his apartment back up the motorway far from us. After a late-night call with him, hearing his loneliness, I called out to the archangels for someone, anyone to help him find his enlightened heart, his spirit once again. I reached out to friends and family in Auckland, desperate for someone to help him find his peace. I knew I did not have the language for him.

Soon after my beautiful healing haven had been built, we took a holiday together to visit William's family in Brisbane. He met up with the guy who ran the local franchise of his own business he had run for more than twenty years in Auckland. They got on well, and the owner said that he would dearly love to retire as he had given it thirty years of his life. This ignited William, and I could see the fire in his eyes. Although it broke my heart to leave my newfound Narnia, home, and loving community in Tauranga, I hoped that a fresh start and his desire for us to be a family again would heal him. He seemed happy and excited, and it was a joy to see him this way.

In more than twenty years of business, no one had ever talked to us about buying our business. But you guessed it. The week we got back from Australia, out of the blue we received a phone call from a friend who sold businesses asking if there was ever a possibility we would consider selling. The universe had done it again, sorted out the details. William's business and where he had placed his heart and great love for most of his adult life was gone into another man's hands, and he could now focus on another new adventure.

I said good-bye to Tauranga and my gentle soul tribe with a lump in my throat and much sadness but felt that moving up to Brisbane would give us a whole new chapter where we could invent ourselves. A tropical life in a hot climate where we could hear the bats dancing and screeching in the fig trees outside our bedroom window, laying back listening to the giant mosquitos humming like low-flying bombers. I was excited about this new opportunity to reinvent us, to become something free and new and to begin a new Angels Rest amongst the kookaburras. William missed the beautiful relationships he had with his male friends and his clients back home who were as close as brothers. The people in Queensland took longer to trust new people.

The children took some settling but enjoyed the adventure, the new accents, the creatures, wallabies down the driveway and toads in the garden causing squeals and nervous laughter. I began to slowly build a new Angels Rest clinic, and the people came. I found once they experienced how it felt to let go of the pain they were carrying, they came back and back and brought family and friends. Once a Queenslander trusts you, they trust you.

There was still so much unspoken between us in our relationship. It was lonely in this new city for Will, although I was meeting so many new people, likeminded souls—fierce, awake, and interesting women but few men. I woke one day with a vision of a woman. I could feel she would help Will somehow, help him be extraordinary.

One afternoon soon after that, we got a message to go and pick up one of our children from a gathering. As I was in the middle of doing homework with our son, I asked Will to go. He went pale and looked at me oddly. He shook his head. "I'm not going," he said.

"Why ever not?" I asked.

"I don't know," he said. "I just feel weird about going. There's something bothering me about it."

Will and I have always tried to help each other push past fear barriers as we see them pop up. We have found that the mind or body can feel threatened by new experiences that could challenge old identities about yourself, and resistant feelings will try to stop you from going outside your comfort zone. We understand though that in order to keep evolving and letting go of old stories that limit, you have to push through. I looked at him and said, "I think there's a reason you're meant to go. I can feel it. Just go."

Three hours later, Will had not come home, and as it was getting dark. I began to pull the curtains, and then I fell to my knees. I felt like I had been punched in the stomach. I saw the vision of the woman in my head again, and I knew that this would be a powerful impact upon our lives, someone who would help bring Will back to his big, beautiful self and away from confusion, from trauma, but I also felt something rip in my heart. I could not explain it, but I knew that something big was happening to us, to him, an ending of something.

When Will came back later that evening, his eyes were shining. He said he had met an amazing human being with real passion for helping people. They had played multiple games of chess and shared some good red wine together. He said he felt like he had always known her.

So, a soul smash. You know when you have experienced one because as you look into their eyes, you just know each other, a sense of having known each other for lifetimes. There is an instant ease, a sense of humor, an "aha" moment. I have long ago let go of believing that this kind of feeling is only possible with a single person, "the love of your life." I believe that especially now, in this time of a great shift in conscious awakening, many of us are meeting many very special people with something to offer who will make us become more genuinely who we are, and these soul smashes are happening all the time. These connections inspire a knowing that you have something important to share. Often you will find yourself saying, "Have we met before?" Or, "How do I know you?" These relationships can be romantic, friendship, or just there to irritate you into recognizing something about yourself. These connections can last forever or for two minutes, but they are profound.

And so it began. They were very excited about each other, and I found myself stuck, just watching and not knowing quite what to do. I think I reverted to my own earlier trauma patterns. I didn't trust my emotions to scream and yell, to head into fight or flight. I simply chose to become a statue to what was happening—a possum in the headlights. I had left my old world behind, moved countries, and had my children and a fledgling business to nurture. I did not yet have the income to move out and manage on my own. I am not someone that ever responds dramatically, and I did not want to go back home to New Zealand. So weighing all that up, and the fact that finally there was someone that was taking William out of the unhappiness he had been in for so long, the only option I felt I had was to accept and allow what was happening right in front of me. Lean into the discomfort and try to be okay with my partner falling in love with someone else.

This woman took Will out of the pain and trauma he had carried since the home invasion and into a new way of seeing life. She helped him heal. For me, I knew that if I loved him unconditionally, I should be excited to see him get his mojo back. In my heart though, I felt abandonment and rejection, and it hurt like hell. I had lost my husband to someone else.

I had not quite expected the person I had called out for when asking the universe for help with William to come in such a powerhouse package. Her strong, powerful way of speaking, physicality, and sexual energy were overwhelming, and the way Will's whole being lit up when he spoke about her was painful. Her performer personality helped William shift out of his old fears, but it was a language and behavior foreign to me, so I did what I could to distance myself and poured all my energy into my work.

I did try to talk to them both in the beginning. To help them understand that I needed them to be thoughtful of my feelings and that the best way to do this would be to allow a friendship to unpack slowly, but they were both too intense to listen.

I knew that I was losing Will to this force of nature although he continued to tell me that I was his heart, he would never leave me, and I could not be replaced. So much within me wanted to tell him to let his connection with her go, to send her away, but I couldn't say it. I knew that he was more alive around her, and for me there was a sense of relief of not being the only one responsible for holding space for his anxiety and trauma.

William is a powerful personality and only sleeps three or four hours a night. Many nights a week, he would wake me to discuss amazing concepts and spirituality. I was exhausted by it, and to have more space where he had someone else to share that with offered me freedom to enjoy the beautiful tropical environment I was living in and to expand myself into my own learning, yoga, teaching, and new friendships, so I said nothing.

So I moved from a monogamous marriage to being with someone who was now a firm believer in polyamory. I could understand about releasing from the ownership and expectation model of many marriages. How for many people the weight of this enmeshed expectation and ownership is so heavy that 60 percent have hidden extramarital affairs. What they were exploring was not hidden, and I was assured by both of them that our relationship would not be threatened. I also began to question my own ideas of monogamy and wondered how it would be to connect physically with someone else. William and I discussed releasing each other of the vow of marriage in spirit without any need to do anything legally and decided it would be more of a loving model for both of us to simply choose to walk together day by day without the weight of marriage. I had stopped wearing a ring daily for a long time, but now I truly put it away, for good.

As we grow up, we are taught to only be freely connected with one person romantically, our partner. I tried to join their flow of understanding of a greater expanded version of love, but I could not stop my mind, body, and heart from being triggered, although I learned to hide it better and better as the months went by. Perhaps it would have helped if I had also found someone else, someone to make me feel special and adored too.

Then one night, things changed. Meeting up with Will and his lady and some other friends at a bar for the Melbourne Cup night in 2014, I looked around the room and saw so much beauty in all the colorful dresses, race day hats, and playfulness. I looked across the room and saw a tall man with shoulder-length hair like a mane. He stared right back at me in his handsome gray suit. I felt a warm rise of desire in my chest and looked over at Will and his lady making lovers' eyes at each other and decided *screw it*. I was sick of being the third wheel.

We started talking, and he told me he was heading off to Sweden to live and work in a few days. He was in his late forties, handsome, strong, a powerful character who had lived a rich and bohemian life. Will's girlfriend had gone home, and it was just the three of us talking, although the chemistry between the man and me was intense. I got up and met Will coming back from the bar and looked him in the eye and asked him to go home. I told him that I wanted to have some time alone with this man, that I needed this and he should go. He looked at me twice, shook his head in amazement, and then left.

I asked the guy to head outside for a walk, and we walked along the side of the river, sharing tales of our lives. He was leaving the country, and after tonight I would never see him again, so I got lost in the moment, the very present connection with him. He kissed me up against the side of a tree, and I lost myself in enjoying his body and his strong energy. We did not make love, but feeling his physicality and feeling sexy and desired felt so good. It had been a very long time since I had felt beautiful this way.

When I got back home in the early hours of the morning, I met a very triggered and unhappy William sitting up in bed waiting for me. He saw that it was not nice being on the other side of your partner exploring someone else, and he was fearful and angry. I assured him that I had not made love to the guy and that I would not be seeing him again; it was something that I needed to find out, and I did not regret it. After that night, William became more respectful of how he was around me with his lover, returning their relationship to a more work focus and friendship; love became more hidden, although he was still utterly in love with her.

When you see someone you love having an intense emotional connection with someone outside your primary relationship, those classic feelings of fear of being alone, of being replaced, of failing in the comparison of beauty stakes, of feeling no longer desirable, of jealousy, of being humiliated, seen as a fool by others you care about—they all raise their ugly heads. For me, as each of those feelings jumped in my belly, in my heart, I battled with them, felt them dance inside me, and then I did my best to release them, to say *no* to each of them. I could not carry these feelings, so I just tried to bury them deeper and spend more time focused on my work or in the hot room in intense yoga.

Sometimes as I walked, or more like crawled through one of these feelings, it felt like death. A lot of people began to notice the strength of the connection between Will and his girlfriend. The posts on social media made it clear what was going on, and I began to get a lot of comments from others, concerned or worried that I was being foolish, naïve, or blind. To each of them I said that I felt that she was a good person for him, who brought him so much healing. I did not like the idea of waving the wife ownership and control red flag over his head. I couldn't do that to him and risk him resenting me for it, and I also found that I could not leave. I was stuck.

With so much of Will's energy focused elsewhere, it forced me to look deeply at myself—to find out who I was outside unity or marriage with him. I realized that I was not living in my own full power. The woman's sheer force meant I had to stop walking next to or even nearby to Will, and I poured all my energy into my healing work. I did more acts of service I came here to do, taking clients on beautiful seaside healing retreats, running meditation classes and seeing clients in my beautiful healing space, the new Angels Rest.

The miracles poured into the room. People would come in intense pain and leave without it. I saw an elderly lady with a great scar on her leg release the hobble and dance down the stairs. I have lost count of the amount of people who have released migraines, back pain, addiction, and abuse. It is always exquisitely beautiful to witness someone releasing what they thought was unforgiveable from their bodies, minds, and hearts and find space within once again. I have worked with army veterans who have freed themselves of PTSD, mothers with postnatal depression once more connected with their own bodies and with their babies, and babies with colic unwind trauma and learn how to sleep. It is a great privilege doing what I love, what I adore, and holding people in a space of unconditional love.

Having more space to myself offered me the opportunity to fully invest myself in my work, healing, writing blogs, poetry, and teaching others. I began teaching corporate groups and yoga classes how to release stress from their minds and bodies through guided meditation, where I would have the whole room in a deep, wide space of calm. I knew I was seeing one of the visions I had seen in the MRI scanner. I also knew one of the reasons for having this experience of being more on my own was to step into my own fullness, my own power rather than constantly looking to my partner for identity. I began to embrace the idea of being more of a lioness—stronger, more powerful, and vital. Okay about speaking my truth, my vulnerabilities and owning my space. I began to see that the most powerful job I had was to be of service with my gift, to share it and help others share theirs.

I moved my focus from one-on-one work with people at Angels Rest and began to also teach larger groups, taking a whole room through the healing process by guided meditation. In this space, I believe we can make different choices at a deep cellular level of how our mind, body, emotions, and spirit are presenting.

We can let go and create profound shifts at a genetic level when we lay back, relax, and enter a meditative space. There is a body of scientific knowledge that explores this, led primarily by the amazing Professor Bruce Lipton called epigenetics. It explores how we get to create our expression of health and genetic expression by what we think—how what we think creates chemical changes in our body, and these chemical changes create or dis-create health.

I find this fascinating, and I love that there is some science behind the work I am doing, so that I am not presenting as some strange clairvoyant healer lady but simply holding space for people to create profound healing in their own bodies by sublimely letting go and letting their internal chemistry do what it does best—find health.

———

I continued to accept the relationship between my partner and his girlfriend for well over a year. Somehow I believed that because there was nothing hidden, it made it more of an advanced and enlightened connection that I should be okay with. The problem was I wasn't okay with it; I wasn't okay with being in relationship with someone who was enmeshed with someone else. I wasn't okay being in a relationship where I felt third; with two people who were not being kind or thoughtful of my feelings or of my heart.

I met a soul smash of my own, a man I connected with as friends and briefly as lovers. Our romantic connection did not last long, and it wasn't meant to. We are better friends and could help each other more beautifully in that space. I deeply listen to others in my work. It is rare that anyone asks me how I am, and if they do, I swiftly deflect the question. This man was different; his ability to listen to me and ask the right questions really helped me see that how I was living in my relationship wasn't empowering.

One night, I decided that I needed to release myself from the pain of my enmeshed relationship with William. I just couldn't do it anymore, and without drama, meanness, or arguing, we discussed separation. I felt a deep sense of relief wash through me and was happy that we could agree to continue to share the home with separate houses on the property and get on with being loving parents to our kids and much better friends without the weight of partnership when I was feeling so abandoned and disappointed in that realm. We forgave each other for all the pain and discomfort we had caused and began to work together on being amazing and real, genuine soul-based friends.

For the last few years, we had both forgotten our wedding anniversary. We had long come to the conclusion that the weight of the marriage contract was not something that we wanted to be bound to. It seemed farcical to celebrate our anniversary while Will was in love with someone else, and then recently something changed in the way we kindly saw each other. We took a trip to Fiji together with our children. During that time, we talked and found a way back to our individual sovereign power, with a new respect for who we were as individuals—not partners, not parents, just people. We decided that we would like to work more together and began to create a retreat program called Unplugged. This program would help people deeply unpack situations and experiences in their lives holding them back. It felt good and exciting to be working in the same soul space together again.

Not long after our trip away, the date of our anniversary came up. For the first time in years, I felt the desire to celebrate our friendship, our comradeship in our constant search for growth as people. I bought him a friendship card and a small gift. Later that day, I came home to find a bunch of flowers in my house, a beautiful handcrafted vanilla candle, and a card that read: *To Veronica, thank you for 4383 days of love.*

We are not here long enough to hold grudges and stay angry. I do love William and always will, but this unconditional love I now feel between us is more powerful than the restricted married love that expected so much before. All the hurt and pain between us is gone—forgiven and no longer attached to our connection. Now, I feel that if he said he was off to Peru for three years to take a self-healing journey, I would support that. If he chose a lover who was kind and gentle and sweet with our children, then great! Our connection is unusual but magical. I am grateful for it.

I like the description of platonic intimacy to describe the new way of connecting with people on the same wavelength—a way I live. This means no guard up or armor; instead, immediate deep vulnerability. There is often a lot of touch with hugs and hand holding and deep care but not taking advantage of people's gentleness. I have several key friendships like this in my life and have no problem telling people I love them. It's very freeing.

What doesn't work with platonic intimacy is needy or craving energy in your body toward the other person. These relationships can be the most powerful connections you have ever experienced. But enjoy them lightly. Don't let the body take over and smash your chance of the gift you can offer each other. Attachment doesn't work. These are not relationships that can handle ownership or expectation.

Sometimes these miraculous beings, these mirrors to our souls, are just not meant to be with you for long—just long enough for you both to get it. To give and receive a beautiful gift of remembering and exploring a fresh start around your heart, your bones, and your skin. I have learned to be profoundly grateful for the positive interrupt these people bring into my life. Even if the moment was only for a heartbeat, a short moment in time, I now see how precious we are in these soul smashups. They offer us the power and intimacy of an unconditional "being seen," and it leaves you changed, able to bring that gift into all the new connections you now have.

Angels Rest our home and my clinic sprawls like a great tree house above the river and has become a place where beautiful and intuitive souls gather. Here I live, work, and teach others how to hold space for healing, how to use their listening ears and unconditionally loving, healing hands to do the work so more of us can remember our natural balance of health and soul-level beauty.

I have a loving circle of warm friends who are healers. We help each other expand and explore limitations that stop us from rising into a place of deep service to the world and keep each other accountable if we see one of us getting lost in spiritual ego, dogma, and drama. We laugh a lot, at ourselves. It feels good.

It feels more real to me to live this way, connecting genuinely with big-hearted friends I care about around me. To love without need for anything other than the divine presence of sitting together and speaking the truth that unlocks broken pieces and heals so beautifully.

Many of my friends are a variety of ages, most of them almost twenty years younger, but all are interested in leaving the world better for having lived in it. What makes us soul tribe family is our ability to crash through the discomfort, say the raw truth, see the painful blocks to change, and shift anyway.

It just means that in this incredible moment of "seeing" and feeling each other, you can share a profound, sacred, human moment of awareness, an unconditional love meant to awaken you to a higher level of consciousness.

The way I live now is so dramatically different from my life before my scars—the scars of cancer and the scars of living a mind-first reptilian existence, as I did for much of my early life, and even the scars of living in a painful relationship. I no longer look to others to come up with the solutions for my life. I have grown up. Finally. I know how to get on with doing what I came here to do. Not perfectly but just the best I know how each day that I am breathing.

I have a spiritual soul mate, good friend, and co-parent who I am no longer married to but who I will always love. I am free to invent my day, and I am not afraid to be vulnerable and real. I have nothing to prove.

The scars on my breast so carefully tattooed into a new nipple and the scar along my back where my muscle was taken to make a new breast have faded into silvery lines. My body is transforming into strength and compassion through writing and poetry, meditation, yoga, breath, healing work, and love. I know that my mind and body still resist shifting, still battle to climb outside of my comfort zone. Sometimes I wonder how I will shift forward. Sometimes I just want to crawl into a cave and get very quiet.

I teach a yoga class to music and candlelight along with guided meditation for a local studio. Not that long ago, I found myself wondering if I should give it over to one of the younger new teachers, someone who has a stronger, more precise way of practicing. I noticed myself having these thoughts as I looked at myself naked in the mirror. My mind came up with all the reasons why I should hand over my teaching role, and then I began to laugh. Instead, I turned up at my class and smiled at all the different shaped and sized brave bodies around me and put my hand on my belly. I said that my belly shows that I have cradled three babies in my arms. The scar on my back and the implant in my breast means that when I bend down and look in the studio mirror, one breast goes sideways.

By sharing my vulnerabilities, I felt free. I told the room that I come to yoga to heal myself from the cells out. That I come to yoga to leave old, stinky feelings on the floor, that every day I practice, my body releases old broken-down stories in cartilage, muscle, and bone and remembers gently how to find healing. I think I loved myself just a wee bit more after that class, and I have never seen a class dance and wiggle their hips more with me between postures.

Each person I work with in the clinic, in the yoga studio, or away on retreat fills me with so much joy. Knowing that everyone has the right to drop pain and find their deep inner love keeps me going. Being of service to others is first. My heart fills to see people's joy in discovering the inner treasure chest of the heart and how they transform mind, body, and soul as a result.

I believe that humans are born beautiful, and we only learn to be distrustful, angry, unhappy, sick, and full of despair due to the stories, events, and trauma that comes at us. At any moment in time, we can lay these feelings down and reclaim our natural birthright for health and well-being. Nothing is held in stone when it comes to health. The human spirit is crazily amazing and can do miraculous things when given half a chance.

I love to teach people how to lay back and relax their bodies and let go of the dramas and pains they have laid upon themselves since birth. So many people I work with are still carrying the shock of an aggressive, too bright, invasive birth. Often I take them back in time by gently imagining a different way of entering this world. Imagining everyone calm, low lights, a calm, relaxed mother, and all those attending being peaceful, respectful, and gentle. I help them see a different possibility, of feeling held and protected, cord not cut too quickly. By imagining profoundly beautiful eye contact with their mother and knowing they are welcomed, a precious gift to the planet, it clears so much birth trauma and life pain.

The body does not know the difference between the stories that happened and replacing it during deep meditation with one that is far more graceful. I have seen much trauma removed from people I have worked with over the years by forgiving the ones who hurt them and then going back and "redoing" the story in a positive way. Being grateful for their body, their heart, and their gentle presence in the world calms a stressed, uncomfortable body. It is a joy to see people's health and well-being transformed this way, as it was for me.

My faith is not religious. Not ordered. Not controlling. My God is love, unconditional love. Every being on this majestic living planet has a birthright to love. Feeling this love that connects us all as brothers and sisters has freed me to be present in my life. This awareness of our loving, vulnerable essence has cleared much of the mind-based pain that used to cause me anxiety and despair, and yet I am aware that every day I still search my less positive reactions and observe why they are there, to release them and let go.

There are a couple of statements I live by that help me stay on path.

You spot it, you got it!

If something is making me itchy and frustrated, I look at how, why, and when the thing I am experiencing is something I am or have created. I look at how I might be resisting life or playing out an old program with people. This keeps me accountable to getting lost in egoism and "poor me" stories.

A fantastic line by the whisky-fuelled Captain Jack Sparrow from the *Pirates of the Caribbean* movie is another line I love.

> *The problem is not the problem. The problem*
> *is your attitude to the problem.*

No matter how bad the situation, there is no reason to activate into fury and lose my cool. I know that when I do this I am a volcano and scary to all around me. It serves no one and nothing, and it is just simple stress activation from my cave-woman basic brain leaving me holding my club and roaring! I can be calmly strong and determined but not nasty, not judgmental, not cruel or mean. It never serves.

I have learned from painful experience that I must be wise and awake to the timing when helping people. Sometimes the reason why they are in pain or the energetic story that can help them let go of their discomfort is all I can hear in my mind when I am with them. If they are not ready to face that part of themselves, and I bring it up, it is like a kick in the face and can trigger a ferocious kick. I try to listen now more than I speak.

I do not judge the girl and woman I was before my scars. The confused girl who had steel armor around her heart and body, the girl who only operated as a walking brain. Although it makes me sad to remember the woman who was so wrapped up in unreal drama she couldn't see or feel the ones around her that loved her, who was so disconnected to her body that she wanted to die. Without the earlier me, the distrustful me, the disassociated me, the diseased me, the fearful escapist me doing all the crazy stuff I've done, I wouldn't be here, and I would not have earned the right to help the people I do every day.

It took me a long time to stop running away from the "past me" and kicking her to the curb. To stop criticizing or running from the older versions of me. I now embrace my vulnerability and write about it as much as possible in blogs or poetry. I tell people how I feel when I feel it. The more I share my discomfort, the more I free myself. The more I free others. These words helped:

How do you know what you are ...
until you know what you are not?

I was woken night after night for a long time being told to write this book—to grow this project past one book into many. When I was given the *Made Beautiful* name in a dream, I knew it would bring people together to share the profound insights their life scar stories had brought them. The twenty-two women who gave me their stories for this book were meant to be in here. The intention is powerful. None of us are meant to be perfect. We did not come upon this planet for this reason. We came here to experience a rich life full of laughter and tears, of joy and despair, of birth and grief, of life. All of it in its messy glory! The scars make us more able to love as we see how vulnerable life is.

This is the time of the great shift. There is a spiritual awakening happening to many of us. What this means is that we are moving out of the ego and the cookie-cutter ways we have thought we have had to live into a more vulnerable truth, living in our individual gift. When you are driven by a desire to live gift or service first, life can become pretty wonderful. Each one of us has something to give this planet and each other. We are not just about keeping a tidy house, tidy children, tidy relationships, a tidy career, and a tidy-looking body; our souls are crying out to be seen and heard, to be what we came here to be, and it's getting louder!

Sharing the hidden wells we hold within us of what has hurt us heals us deeply. It also heals others and helps them understand that they too can be vulnerable and beautiful.

If you are reading this, look within. Are there scars or wounds unresolved? If so, I urge you to get out your journal or your laptop and begin to write your own story. The story that only you can tell in your most perfect *you* language and then share it with us so we can see you and hear you and hold you in your sharing at www.madebeautifulbyscars.com

By sharing your raw truth, you will see that you are loved, accepted, and found to be more than okay. It will make you feel fierce and free as a human, and that is an awesome feeling!

We are made beautiful by scars.
With love,

Veronica

Kate Cornfoot Photography

Amanda's Story

When I first moved to the town where Amanda and her family live, I heard about this inspiring woman. She had only recently had her accident, and the community came together with so much love to support her and her beautiful family. A couple of dear friends had helped set up evenings to gather financial support for the family, joyful nights full of dance and laughter, music, delicious soup, and so much love. So many people were drawn to lovingly support them where they could. Amanda is a true inspirational force of nature and has touched more people than most of us ever do in a lifetime. She is hope. She is fierce. She is power.

It was late summer 2013 when I dove off my surfboard without my hands up. It was something I always did. But I hit a sandbar and broke my neck. It was six days after the birth of our daughter Ziggy, a sister for three-year-old Lola.

I heard the crunch. I was face down in the water. I tried to push myself up, but my arms and legs wouldn't work. I was strangely calm and knew nothing would ever be the same. In that moment, I decided that if worse came to worst, I'd breathe in water. I'd heard it was a better way to go, but for some reason I didn't think that would happen.

I'd been at the beach with a Spanish friend Miguel and my little girl Lola. We were surfing while we waited for a paraglide off the mountain. I'd sworn to my partner Gemma that I'd just show him a good time for a couple of days. Then I'd be by her side looking after her and our new bub.

Now I was helpless, facedown, holding my breath. In my head, I was calling out, "Look up Miguel! Look up Miguel!" Then I felt myself being turned over. I could see the sky, I could breathe, and I wasn't dead. Miguel cradled my head in his elbows with his hands under my armpits and pulled me gently through the water toward the beach. Other people had stopped to help, and they put me on my surfboard and dragged me up the sand. Someone called an ambulance. I could hear Lola crying out for me in the background.

Everything was so clear. In the emergency department, I remember telling the crew not to cut my bikini because I really liked it and somehow thought that I'd be wearing it again next week.

The day before, I'd been climbing down naked from Lola's top bunk. I'd looked at my body; it was brown and six-packed. I thought to myself it was a good body, a strong body. I loved my life. Every day I'd think how blessed I was, and I made the most of the incredible environment we lived in. I was in the water rain, hail, or shine, either kite-surfing or stand-up paddle boarding, and I rode my bike everywhere, usually with Lola between my arms.

For twenty years, I'd been a chef, half of them as owner operator of my own thriving cafe/restaurant. I'd traveled the world, worked on super yachts, walked 840 kilometers across Spain in the Camino de Santiago, was a gardener, a yogi, a motorbike rider, and kite-surfer. The future was exciting, as I'd just begun the transition to a new career in academia with the completion of my master's.

A new life began the moment I broke my neck. I suffered a 110 percent anterior dislocation, with C6 coming to rest in front of C7. But my spinal cord didn't rip or tear; instead it stretched like a bungee. The medical diagnosis is that I am tetraplegic (all four of my limbs are affected). I am paralyzed from my chest down. No bladder or bowel control, no core, no legs, and hardest of all, my hands don't work.

My physical reality feels like I'm sitting on a Swissball with my feet off the ground. I have no center and no balance, with the stability of a newborn. At the spinal unit, I couldn't hold my hand above my head without it falling, couldn't sit without wanting to pass out. I remember feeling absolute fear when sitting on a bench, with my feet on the ground, having to lean forward toward the ground. Something so simple, that I'd done millions of times before, two weeks after injury made me want to vomit. That drop looked as big as the Grand Canyon.

Others told me that I'd get my head around it, as that would be my new point of strength and balance. From this position, I could have some independence. With my nose on my knees, using my legs as a fulcrum, I would be able to transfer between my chair and other surfaces without help. It felt like an impossible goal.

Luckily reality sinks in slowly like a leaf falling from a tree. From the early days of feeling like you are on a crazy roller coaster where all you can do is firefight, to two years on where you can say … so this is it.

At a crisis point (often brought on by injury or illness), the old you is erased. You are changed forever, and so are those around you. When I got slammed, everybody in my circle was rocked. It didn't fit in their schema of the way the world was supposed to work. They've told me that it's made them grateful, made them get off their butts, to push themselves, to live more fully. They tell me I'm their reason—"Amanda would if she could"—and they're right!

If you'd asked me who I was prior to injury, I would have pointed to my body and said, "This is me." I was 80 percent physical. Now all I can say is that I am. Ego has been stripped away. Now my reality is not so much about my physicality but my presence. Unlike before, I'm here, I'm in the moment, I pay way more attention, whereas before I'd be looking over your shoulder at the wind, to see if I could go kiting. I know now that I am not my body. For me, it is now an intellectual, emotional, and spiritual journey—an ultra marathon of the soul.

When I think about my old life, it's like the death of a friend. Two years on, and I still miss her but can't wish her back. I'm grateful to her for providing the strong foundations on which to build the new me—an established spiritual practice and a strong body and mind.

There are still moments of grief, anger, and sadness when I kick myself for even being at the beach. When I think about how different my kids' life would be with two able-bodied parents. How it would feel to be able to pick them up and feel them against me, to lean over them at night and tuck them in. I think about how hard it is for Gemma and how much I want to hold her, or let her sleep in, or even just make her a cup of tea. These moments of acknowledging what has been lost reinforce how lucky I am to be alive. I have a gorgeous young family and an incredible partner. I have to use everything I have to engage in the world ... find creative ways to bring joy ... to find joy ... to play ... to set an example for our kids ... to be there for Gemma. I've not yet achieved all that I think is possible in this crazy new body, but I'm still trying.

From early on in my injury, I began to explore what I had left to work with. I meditated daily, visualized my body, and tried to feel it, connect with it. But how do you connect and care for what you can't feel, when nothing is the same? With other people helping me with every aspect of my physical life, it would be easy to hand over that care. But I know in my heart that I have to keep loving all of me, touching and paying attention so the existing pathways won't die—while hopefully making new ones. I believe in neuroplasticity! I believe the brain is responsible for the change that happens in the body, and I'll never stop trying to bring change and be more.

I swim, do yoga, and play wheelchair rugby. It was while playing wheelchair rugby that I forgot I was in a chair; I was having so much fun (what a gift). I want to go hard ... be rough ... compete ... I didn't realize how important it would be to roll into a space where people with legs are the odd ones out! There is an unspoken understanding and camaraderie when we hang out with other "wheelies" that helps my family create a new normal.

I've kite-surfed strapped to my crazy friend, who is brave enough to tie himself to a seventy-two-kilogram, living, breathing piece of concrete. The wind, the waves, and the speed feel the same. It's total joy to feel the freedom that I thought was gone forever! And, as the first tetra in the world to do it, hopefully it will encourage others along the way to follow their passion.

Before the accident, I was so busy being human that I would never have known that my real strength was never from my body. Despite only having 14 percent function, who I am remains unchanged. The worst moments in our lives make us who we are. We forge meaning. We choose moment by moment who and how we want to be in the world.

Kate's Story

I first met Kate not long after moving to Brisbane. Gentle Kate and her babe arrived one morning at Angels Rest, and they were beautiful to work with. In my clinic, I see many mothers struggling with mothering. Not Kate. The bond between her and her sweet son filled the room with so much love and palpable warmth. Her journey has helped her see the exquisite space in the heart of the moment. I think you would agree it has left a lasting gift in her photography. The first photo below was taken one year before the one beneath it. This second photo takes my breath away. Kate's deep wisdom and extraordinary beauty is powerfully seen here, pouring from her eyes.

Photography by Kate Cornfoot

*W*hen the skin specialist sat me down in her office, I knew from the look on her face it was bad news.

"You have a melanoma. It has to be removed as soon as possible. You're lucky we caught it early."

I immediately went to the most morbid place in my mind, imagining my young children growing up without their mum. But once I let myself feel the grief and the fear, I got on with the next step—surgery.

I was wheeled out of the operating theatre and into recovery. Having had a large superficial section of my cheek removed, I was steeling myself for my husband's reaction. I imagined him reeling back in horror. But he didn't. I then worked up the courage to look at myself in the mirror. The wound was still bleeding, my stitches stood out like angry ants on my face, and a black eye was blooming. It was not the face I knew.

In those first few weeks, I hated my scar. It hurt, it was very swollen and red, and I feared my appearance would scare small children (and it did—my four-year-old daughter was visibly shaken upon seeing me for the first time after surgery). I hid myself behind a shaggy hair cut, big floppy hats, and dark sunglasses. Out of my "disguise" at home, I made jokes about auditioning to play the next Bond villain or a tough inmate on a prison drama. The humor helped a little but also hid the pain I felt about losing my pretty face. But as the physical scar slowly healed, so too did my feelings.

I started to reflect on what I felt I had lost when I'd had surgery. Most obviously, and positively, I lost my skin cancer. I also examined my feelings around losing some of my beauty. I felt I'd lost some of my identity; this new face I saw in the mirror didn't reflect who I felt I was. The turmoil of all these feelings, coupled with the desire to transcend them, pushed me into a new place of acceptance. I didn't have my old face anymore, so I might as well accept (and embrace) the new one!

Over time, my facial scar has become just another bodily change I accept and respect, like my stretch marks from puberty and two pregnancies, the lines on my face as I march into the middle of my thirties, my smaller breasts after breastfeeding two children. They all bear witness to my growth as a person, to the experiences that have challenged me and delighted me, to the miracle that is my ongoing existence. I am alive when others who have had melanoma are not.

These experiences have also found their way into my art, photography. I started out merely capturing the physical changes taking place during the healing process—how I looked the day before surgery, the day after surgery, and then as my scar faded and changed. But as I grew in gratitude and found my sense of humor again, I found myself photographing those ordinary moments in a mum's day—folding laundry, cooking, washing clothes—but with an irreverent twist. For example, one morning as I attempted to put away the 1067th load of washing, I thought to myself, *This would be so much more fun on roller-skates.* I took a photo of it, and it spawned a whole series of humorous images of me being the Playful Housewife. My art and my joy over the simple things in life have combined in this wonderful way as a result of my melanoma journey.

Today, a year after the surgery, I feel beautiful. My scar is now a silvery line most people don't even notice. I marvel at how well my body has healed, and I have a deep appreciation and an immense gratitude for all the learning this experience has given me.

Photography by Kate Cornfoot

Ally's Story

I was drawn to Ally's sensitivity and the raw vulnerability of her posts on Facebook. I felt guided to contact her and ask her to share her story. I am glad I did! Ally is wise beyond her years and is full of a healer's gift. Like many healers, she has experienced pain and the scars of dis-ease in the body. On the road to health, she is exploring what it means to be a healer, and the journey ahead looks wonderful for her.

$\mathcal{A}$ll I have ever wanted to do is to help not just people but animals. It is my calling and my true life purpose. I thought the only way I could ever achieve this was through nursing, and I am eternally grateful for my time as a nurse, as it taught me many lessons.

One of favorite childhood memories I have is being dressed in a nurse's uniform with the plastic stethoscope around my neck. I was convinced I could hear my Nanny's heartbeat. From the moment I put that nurse's hat on, I was convinced that was what I was going to do. Anyone who knows me gets that I am a very determined person and whatever I put my mind toward I achieve, and I did exactly that. I became a registered nurse.

My journey toward nursing was filled with the full spectrum of emotions, from the pain and heartache I witnessed when I saw a husband become a widow in the space of thirty minutes through to being present to the beauty of newborn life and the elation I cannot describe, mixed with fear of *Will this little one-kilogram baby make it out alive?*

So what changed? It took ten years, lots of tears, turning to alcohol, breaking down, and feeling suffocated by this invisible contract between me and the universe that I would spend my life giving back to others in the only way I thought I knew how … nursing. I felt trapped and lost in the dark.

There was something whispering inside of me that I had a story to tell. The whisper grew louder and louder until I had a health scare and life forced me to take time out. Little did I know that during my darkest days of being stuck in bed in a fog, I would learn the art of being kind toward myself.

Life always has a way of putting you in the right direction; it's up to you if you listen to that whisper or wait for life to shout at you.

Over a year ago, I found myself in an ambulance screaming and feeling like my insides were on fire. It turns out it was my ovary twisting on itself from a large cyst that took six months, multiple emergency room visits, countless ultrasounds, and finally an emergency laparoscopy to *get the f****r out …*

This was a very long and arduous road to recovery. It took a lot of faith, patience, and remaining steadfast in knowing my body was trying to tell me something. The pain was crippling, and I was seeing doctor after doctor, searching for answers desperately. I prayed and asked my angels to be there for me and help send me the right treatment.

I felt so scared, but I knew that I was being looked after. I felt the angels' presence as I fought through every day. It took one senior surgeon (after six months) to take one look at me crippled with pain even on a ketamine (horse tranquilizer) infusion, and I was sent into emergency surgery to save my life.

I am on the road to recovery thanks to the unconditional love and support from my amazing partner and her mum and my guardian angels and our tireless effort toward finding a solution.

So in the midst of being in and out of hospital, I was reading self-help books, practicing mindfulness, then eating too much chocolate, watching too much TV for my liking, and feeling like I was merely existing until I could go back to work as a neonatal nurse. But the very thought of having to help put an IV in a baby's tiny veins or watch a mother look helplessly on as her child stopped breathing filled me with fear and resentment.

I made a promise to myself when I started on my journey to be a nurse that the moment I became jaded I would leave, for the greater good of everyone. I continue to be inspired by the incredible team of nurses, doctors, and allied health professionals I have worked with who still selflessly dedicate their lives to saving these precious babies, and being there to help their families through the toughest times they may ever face. It has been an honor and utmost privilege to work with so many amazing people; this is my ode to each and every one of you. Thank you for the knowledge you shared and the wisdom you imparted to me.

We all have the ability to change the course of our life. What I now know is to follow my intuition, embrace my passions, and share my story to help others break out of what they think they are supposed to be doing and instead do what they are meant to be doing. By following your calling and learning to be compassionate to the most important person in your life—you—you get to live a rich and full life.

Nadine's Story

Nadine Lee is a tantra yoga teacher and embodiment coach I met in Bali. She is gifted in seeing potential and is passionate about creating sacred spaces and community for others to awaken to their true essence and innate wisdom. Hers is a very brave and sacred life journey, and I am grateful she allowed her vulnerability to be shared with us as a healing tool for many.

*U*p until the past few years, speaking about my scars was rarely welcomed. Even sitting here writing this piece, I feel into the darkest parts of this journey thus far and think, *Well, some women elsewhere in the world have probably endured suffering way worse than I have.*

As a young girl, I was first sexually violated at the age of six. The emotional scars of the little girl inside me wept for some compassion and tender care. Only now at age twenty-eight I am able to begin to face the wounds of the little girl who was curiously and innocently exploring in the world, only to realize she got herself in some crazy situations, and no one was there to protect her.

"Where were you all? Why are you so tough skinned?"

Vulnerability was seen as a weakness and drummed out of our feminine lineage. However, the vulnerability gene in me appeared too persistent to back down.

The way of coping with deep, repressed pain around feeling unsafe in this world and all of my boundaries being violated was to turn inwards and hide. Pleasure was confusing, because my hypersexual six-year-old self actually enjoyed those feelings of being touched, being special, feeling loved and desired. The guilt I carried for years around this very realization led me to shame and guilt around all aspects of worldly pleasures.

Food was a major one. I loved transferring all my guilt onto food, and I remember dieting from the age of twelve years old. At fourteen, I experienced an incredible psychological phenomena—some psychotherapists called it psychosis or disassociation—whereby my mind literally disappeared, and I was left in a mindless, numb state, not knowing who I was, what was real or not real for three days straight.

After this terrifying experience, I can now relate to it as Kundalini awakening. Others might relate to it as similar to a trip on Ayauhascha or LSD; I was never the same. My body/spirit had split, perhaps to cope with the suppressed trauma as a child. Every day was a struggle, trying to keep it together mentally. Paranoia was an understatement to what I felt. I was convinced people wanted to poison me and that I was being watched. I kept it all "together," acing my classes with top grades at an elite women's Catholic school. No one had a clue what was going on in my head. On the outside, I looked like I had it all together; on the inside, not so much …

Confusion, depression, suicidal thoughts, despair, and aloneness in the worst possible way.

As a seventeen-year-old young woman, I reached rock bottom; my final year of high school, the only thing that kept me together was focusing all my energy into my school studies, and low and behold, I graduated with amazing marks and got into the best university in my state. At the same time, I was clinically diagnosed with depression, depersonalization disassociation disorder, paranoia, and anorexia. But hey, the appearance was most important, right? Keep it together, suck it up, and for God's sake, don't be so sensitive.

When I turned eighteen, it all came out; the truth was revealed. The lies of the sexual abuse that had been swept under the rug and dismissed as "normal" were highlighted by my rage and mass exposure of what happened.

The path to sexual freedom and liberation began consciously on this day.

Unconsciously it began as a six-year-old girl.

Reclaiming My Erotic Innocence and Saying Yes to Pleasure

Wow! This is a theme of society, not just someone who has been sexually violated. What I have realized on this path is that most of us have been cut off from our pleasure, our sexuality and bodies, either through direct trauma or just by living in a world dominated by fear and sexual repression.

The irony of my life is that sex is at the core. Sex got me here, sex broke my connection to God, and now sex has come back as the path back to God.

Retracing my steps back to wholeness, my body was vanishing physically as a physical symptom, my mind in turmoil as a mental symptom, and the antidote was a homeopathic dose of the initial disconnect.

At twenty years old, the anorexia resurfaced, this time even worse. This was the point where my entire life radically transformed. I used to read my own palms as a child and look at the point around twenty to twenty-five years old and know something huge was going to happen around this age.

Basically the same thing happened as when I was fourteen; however, this time I had resources and the inner strength to cope. I found myself on a total mind-body-soul detox. Everything that was not serving me anymore was being radically stripped from my life. Conditionings, cultural constructs, and belief systems all were being rocked. My body was shedding weight like no tomorrow, literally getting prepared for a reset. World-famous healers were suddenly appearing in my life, yoga was my new addiction, and vegan was my preferred diet.

It wasn't until I opened up into the wonderful world of sacred sexuality that everything changed. Finally, going to the core of the eating disorders, the depression, the anxiety took me to nowhere else but within my body. And of all places, in my vagina!

I dived into sessions involving tantric yoni (vagina) massage, vaginal de-armoring, exploring my shadow, owning my pleasure, owning my slut and seductress, and radically breaking down the conditioning at lightning speed. I knew this all had to go, as this life I am here to do big things, and that cannot be in my way. Luckily, being so young, the effects moved quickly, as such practices release deep trauma in the deep subconscious mind, freeing fear, guilt, and shame, awakening the body to life-force energy to purify the entire physical, energetic, and psychic body, allowing pleasure to be reclaimed.

I was on a rapid lightning speed to evolve, things were shifting, and before I knew it my entire life took a 360-degree flip. I quit my glossy magazine job in Sydney to pursue studying alternate therapies. I moved from Sydney to Byron Bay and explored all aspects of relationship, from polyamory to dating a woman. I downsized my life possessions to fit into one backpack, became a full-blown hippy, studied yoga and tantra in India, started my own business, and most importantly, got to know who I truly was. I began to create my life based upon my strengths, my skills, my weaknesses, and my nature, not according to how society had told me to *be*.

What I see is that the illusions of this world are constantly being stripped away and that this life is one big stage to play upon. We are the stars of our very own movie, and we have the power to change our roles and characters whenever we like. Revisiting the initial traumas and scars that take us into the darkest parts of the soul are the key to liberation from them.

Consciously going back into the darkness was where my true light was birthed. Just like a lotus in muddy waters, a vision I often get when meditating and the theme of this current life journey is the darkness and the light are simultaneous. One cannot exist without the other; it is from the dark, muddy waters that the beautiful lotus flower can bloom. The beauty is so beautiful only because it knows the polar opposite of mud and gunk. However, it draws its power and sustenance from below where it's come from, in order to shine bright into the light where it resides now—embracing of every aspect along the way, as it's all perfection in the grand scheme of things.

This is how I see these past experiences, as the fuel and source for all beauty in my life to now be birthed. Every day I am still facing new wounds and scars as the journey to wholeness goes deeper and deeper, and I wouldn't have it any other way.

I only know beauty now because I have seen and lived in the ugly parts of life. I only know compassion now because I have seen fear. What I know is that the middle of all these opposites is a love that has always been there and always will be.

Today I find myself living a life, sharing and inspiring others to also see the beauty amongst the dark. I can only do this because I have come out the other side of my own mud. I feel that the greatest gift we can give others and ourselves is to be of service. Even if we support one person along their path, showing them merely a glimpse of the beauty possible within, our job is done. The ego wants to think we need to create a mass revolution and change the world. No. The world changes as soon as we each do. That one change internally ripples into every single person we touch along the way.

Love,

Lay Down the Stories

by Veronica

Stories screw up the end
Of relationships
    And our hearts.
The stories we tell others and ourselves
About why it ended,
    About why it hurt,
        About the grief, pain, and loss,
            Needs unmet.
These stories create a gray wall of sludge
In our hearts
That color the love
We once had,
The love
    That is still there
        Under it all.
What if we laid down all the stories
    In our book of love
        And instead saw evolving love,
    A spectrum of color
That grew past desire
And moist, enmeshed limbs
To gentle compassion
    And kindness
        From afar?
What if we didn't have to make
Someone wrong
    Or right ...
But just allowed
Shift and transformation
    Gently?
For shift we do,
We all do ...

Wouldn't that be more loving
And bring more gentleness
    To the wounded?
    Create less casualties,
        Less tears?
What if we simply kept our sense of humor,
Released perfection,
And allowed
Misshapen words,
Thoughts, and actions
Without the knee-jerk
    And losing trust in love?
A world without "ex's,"
    More a collection of loved ones
        Like multicolored crystals of various shapes
Who you have been blessed, so honored to hold
    In your beautiful life.
I think there would be more love in that
If we allowed people to be just who they are
    Each day
        Anew
            And
    Let go gently
        With a namaste
    And a gentle smile …

Nicky's Story

*Nicki has written about a pain that many women suffer when battling infertility.
She devotes her life to helping young people and is a beautiful and vulnerable
storyteller of her life scars.*

$\mathcal{T}$he purpose of my writing this is to shed some light and share experiences from the perspective of a woman going through the experience of trying to get pregnant through IVF. An experience that spans a lifetime of three years, four months, and we're still counting. My hope is that this is a raw and real encounter—not to be too serious but more so to normalize the experience for others who may be going through a similar thing. And to show you that you are not alone in this.

The impact that reading about other peoples' experiences had on my journey cannot be underestimated. It helped me immensely. And although everyone's experience will be different and unique, there will likely be some similarities along the way.

For my beautiful wife and I, our experience started in September 2012 with our first doctor's appointment. As of now, January 2016, we are mentally, physically, and financially preparing ourselves for our second round of IVF egg collection. This is not an experience to be rushed (I have learned to accept this); however, pushing thirty-six years old, there are other pressures that are starting to come into play. Nevertheless, it is important to me that this story is a source of inspiration, not sadness. Of strength, not desperation. And of hope, not loss.

Following are journal entries taken ad hoc that give true insight into the trials and tribulations of my personal journey to fulfill my deep desire to be a mum.

Third Time Unlucky—22 Feb. 2014
Journal Entry

We have just gone through the process of completing our third IUI cycle—unsuccessfully. This time is hitting me harder than the first two times. This time I feel really, really sad and maybe a little bit scared as well. The other times it was "only" the first or second try; it was completely normal and acceptable for the insemination not to take. The third time though, I can't help thinking thoughts like, *Am I going to get pregnant? What if there is something wrong with me?* Coupled with the fact that I (and everyone around me) really *felt* like this was it, this was the month. I almost would have bet money on it, that this was the month we would fall pregnant.

It was such a bizarre feeling to think that I was pregnant. When I first found out that we were most likely not pregnant (we took an early detection pregnancy test that came up negative), I felt really silly. I felt stupid and embarrassed for thinking that I was pregnant. That was only for a short while though, before I felt absolutely gutted.

I'm pretty sure there was some denial initially when I was in disbelief and utter disappointment at seeing there was only one line on the test. The next morning, I was completely in denial and decided that I could still very well be pregnant, and I felt good again. Two hours later, I got my period. Sad! I cried a lot and then started questioning myself. Am I too fat to get pregnant? Should I not have drunk that drink (or two) throughout the month?

I have been really good this month, doing a lot of yoga, eating pretty healthy; I've not been stressed at work at all (even though I've had plenty of opportunity to be). I've been really happy and positive and doing a lot of visualizations and reading positive affirmations, but obviously it wasn't enough. I don't actually think that it wasn't; I just think that it takes time. I can't expect to do things well for only a month and then magic will happen. But then again, why not! That is the type of person that I am—think big and always believe in magic. No matter what, I need to not lose sight of this. It can be really hard at times, but I have to believe that it will happen for us.

Yes, I am scared that I won't be able to get pregnant, but that is not what I am to focus on. I need to, and will, keep focused, and I need to believe! We have only had three complete cycles, and it is exhausting. We have also had a number of cycles that didn't make it to the insemination stage. I am pretty good at staying positive, but being third-time unlucky in this cycle—it threw me off course for a bit.

I didn't cope very well with the unsuccessfulness of it. However, it may serve to remind me of all of the positive things that happened this month *because* of going through the cycle. I focused on myself and dedicated real time to nurture and health. I had some seriously inspirational yoga and meditation sessions where I connected to the universe and opened myself up. It was incredible. I was more aware of what I was putting into my body and ate healthier than normal, including cutting out all alcohol and starting a plant-based diet. I have been more dedicated to eliminating bad stress from my life (and better understanding stress and the impact it has on people). For me, it is always easier to do these types of things for the benefit of someone else rather than for yourself. It brought my wife and I even closer as we went through the entire process together. It gave our whole family something to hope for and dream of. We'll break for next month and talk to our doctor about options and then pick up again next month. Until then …

It's a Game Changer—April 2014
Journal Entry

So after a couple of months off to think about things, we have decided to skip straight to IVF. Some people, it feels like more than I realized, opted for this upfront. We wanted the process to be as natural as possible, so we went down the IUI path first. I hate taking tablets and medicines for the sake of it and was really hoping that we would be able to fall pregnant and naturally as possible without any procedure that was too invasive. Well, that plan is out the window, and we are now onto plan B. The fact that we are now onto plan B is somewhat frightening and in some ways upsetting. Mind you, I am grateful that I have a plan B! And the frightening part, well, I have to work through that. I have to get my mind as prepared and ready as much as my body.

The silver lining throughout all of this is that I am now deemed "medically infertile." Yep, you heard it here first. Wow! I am medically infertile. I'm not sure people think about what they are actually saying to a woman when they say this to her. Or if they consider the potential impact that this may have. To be honest, not too much has been explained to me on this one, except for the fact that we will receive financial help. And don't get me wrong that is awesome, and I am really grateful for that, as this is a costly process. But being medically infertile is something far removed from money and finances when you are the person that *is* such a thing. And am I? Can that be determined after only three failed IUI attempts? I mean there is only a 5–10 percent chance of success rate, isn't there? Or was 20–30 percent the latest statistic I heard? But I know that I went into this thinking it was a 16–20 percent chance, didn't I? How am I supposed to be confident about anything if I don't even know statistically what chance I have? Now, I'm sure I read that IVF has a 90 percent chance of success —or was that 20–30 percent?

Now rationally, I know that a statistic can't be totally relied upon and that there are so many variances to each personal situation that impacts a woman's ability to get pregnant (which is probably why there are so many different stats, and clear answers to questions are dodged all over the place). But sometimes, thinking rationally doesn't quite enter the picture—and this is even before the IVF cycle even begins.

So as I brace myself for the journey of IVF, I will have many choices along the way—choices on how I choose to handle things, believe things. Yes, there will definitely be many challenges and, as they say, opportunities to grow. I will take this experience with both hands, and I will give it everything I've got. I will look after my health and myself like I never have before. I will be strong but allow myself the time to be weak when needed.

I will lean on my support group and remember that I am not alone. I will increase the size of my support group, to make sure that I have people to talk to who understand what I am going through. I will not let it take over my life and commit to having a healthy balance in my life despite the continual maternal yearning to have a baby. I will be happy for those around me who are experiencing the miracle of being pregnant and having a child. I will balance positivity and hope as well as being a realist. I will embrace this life experience, a road less walked on (although not rare these days), one that will make me a stronger and more diverse and powerful woman.

With change comes growth, with adversity comes stretching, and with testing comes results. I will do my best to keep some perspective on what is most important—that is family, love, and health (and a bit of laughter along the way).

Out of the Darkness … and into the Light—9 August 2014
Journal Entry

I have spent a good part of this year thinking that I am not going to get pregnant. Preparing myself for the worst. Not getting my hopes up and managing my emotions/expectations. Six months have passed since our last failed attempt to get pregnant.

They took us through everything that I needed to know. The timeframes, the process, the side effects, the costs, and so on. I diligently took lots of notes to refer to later (something I've not actually done yet).

We also saw our counselor, which was great timing, and she gave us some priceless advice, particularly around our doctor.

The basic message I took was not to settle! Do not settle and just accept the way that your doctor works with you. Be honest with yourself, especially if the little things just don't sit right. Sometimes it takes a third party to give you that perspective and let you know that actually that's not okay. Sometimes it's about taking a leap of faith and trusting your instincts. As a nice person, I don't like to upset people or hurt their feelings. As someone who has to face confrontation on a (sometimes daily) basis at work, I don't like confrontation in my home life. So when the doctor asks my wife to step out into the reception area instead of being with me, I see it's time to look around for a new doctor.

Blah, Blah, Blah, Blah, Blah! September 2014
Journal Entry

September 2—I feel blah, blah, blah, blah, blah, blah, blah! I've been on a mental journey since February. We've changed doctors and are preparing for our first IVF egg collection in a couple of weeks. Maybe I'm a bit nervous and scared, and that's contributing to my crappy mood. It's bizarre; we've got a selection of sperm donors to choose from, and we seem to be procrastinating. I wonder why that is. I am so completely unmotivated and uninspired at the moment. I don't know what is coming over me. Or why I'm feeling like this. I feel like I am in an ongoing rotating cycle of constant change and uncertainty. Constant challenges. Nothing seems to get better, and I can't seem to move forward. I feel like I've been saying "we're at the point that everything is going to settle" for the last two years.

September 8—I can't remember if it was last Tuesday or Wednesday, but one of those two days I just couldn't stop crying, I took myself to the doctor and got a mental health plan and am booked in to see my psychologist. I am really looking forward to seeing her. I have worked through a few thoughts of what is upsetting me, and I think it's a combination of a few things, the main one being the baby stuff. It's so hard to be kind to yourself sometimes. It's the same old story. I'm being weak. Am I overreacting? Am I being stupid? It's sending me crazy. People keep saying that I can't help what I feel and therefore it's valid.

Of course that's true—when it's somebody else. But it is so much harder to swallow when it's you. It's like the ad hoc panic attacks that I have. I have everything a fortunate and rich person could ever have in life. Why would I be crying or having a panic attack? I don't have the right or reason to—it's absurd. Yet it's very real. And then that will tip me over the edge. I never know how a day will go until I am in it. There's no telling until I wake up in the morning.

September 10—Yesterday was a good day. Had a big cry in the middle of the day but just took myself to the park across the road and allowed myself to cry and then did ten minutes of mindfulness meditation. It made a huge difference. I felt so much calmer afterwards, clearer. I had a good afternoon. I am sick of analyzing my thoughts. I'm sick of overthinking things. I actively threw it all out to the universe, and I thought words of kindness to myself. I imagined what I would say to me if I were someone else. I can't remember what I said to myself, but it was obviously good. And it worked.

A Moment of Reflection, How Far We've Come—28 July 2015 Journal Entry

To have a wound in your heart that you never knew could exist. To grieve a loss but not just any loss—a loss of something you are unsure that you even had in the first place. The confusion and uncertainty that come with this can seem, at times, almost unbearable. The self-doubt that joins this scenario is an entity of its own. But you can't succumb to the self-doubt, nor the confusion or the uncertainty. This is your chance to stand up. To be the powerful, beautiful, bold woman that you are.

For me, it was having a sneak peak into feeling the power of a mother's love and then to have it taken away before I even had a chance to explore its full depth, its full meaning and the full extent of its purpose. For me, it was the giving of a mother's love and the receiving of a child's embrace in return. Building on the amazing family that I already had (wonderful partner and fur-babies) by filling the space of children in our loving home. The thought crossed my mind that maybe I was being greedy, wanting too much in this journey taking us through the roads of doctors, donors, injections, tablets, crazy hormones, and landing us on the doorstep of IVF. In the meantime, we were presented with the opportunity to be a family support and proxy parents to a young person in need.

The stars aligned, and the timing was perfect. There was an instant connection, and I felt so blessed. Our family was whole. We had one child join our family, and a possible other was on its way, albeit through a grueling IVF cycle. It was truly a blessing. Our home was filled with love and laughter. It was filled with the essence of family.

Somewhere along the way, things changed, and they were not as they had seemed. Sadly we had an early miscarriage, and there were bumps in the road with our "son," which changed the dynamics of our family relationship dramatically. The family structure we had initially embarked on was not the reality, and I had to pull back on the motherly love I had so freely given. This was a heartbreaking state of affairs for me. I felt lost and didn't know my role, my way, or what I was expected to do. The pain of reaching out to love, nurture, and support a child with all of your being, only to have it pushed away, rejected even, was painfully real. And coupled with the timing of our miscarriage, this pain/heartbreak reached new heights. It was as though my heart lay uncovered, fully exposed, with my soul bare and the eagerness to give all that I had and all that I have only to find that it was not enough. It was like a torture, a torment, and a cruel joke of some kind, only I can't hear who might be laughing.

To feel such loss, let alone two losses at once, was heartbreaking. I questioned the validity of this "loss" and my right to feel it. After all, I had barely been pregnant, and our relationship with our proxy child was still fairly new. I had held in my hand and nurtured in my heart the true love a mother would give a child only for it to be taken away so quickly. It made me wonder if it was real or if I'd dreamt it up. Would it be too much for me to describe my hurt as a scar on my heart that heals and then opens again to the oddest of touch or sound or feeling or thought?

What scared me the most is that it might never happen. I might feel this hole and this yearning for an eternity. This might be the way that life is meant to be for me. I look at other families, and the raw truth of it is that mostly it is with love and happiness, yet other times I look upon them with sadness and envy. Might I admit that? It is true. Does that make me a bad person? No, it makes me human.

Despite this human element, a fear of who I might become rises in me, as I don't want to fall into a typical cliché of desperation or sadness for being childless. Even as I write these words, I can feel a shift and a change in me. I don't believe it will be true; however, it still sits on my shoulder. Perched on the back of my neck. Just in case, waiting to say I told you so. Maybe this is your one pain. Maybe this is your burden or cross to bear. Nobody's life can be that perfect.

We all have a story, and this is mine.

———

This is what I felt in the darkest corner of my heart, in the darkest part of the night. When the world was fast asleep and I would toss and turn with fears, torments and hurts.

Through nurturing and nourishing my mind, my body, and my soul, I have, and continue to, work through the pain. Through learning to love myself unconditionally and allowing myself the space to feel this pain as raw and harsh as it is at times. To find the means within me to cut the heartstrings that held onto it for dear life. And to have the ability to sit with it for just long enough in order to release it and let it go.

It takes time, it takes courage, and it takes strength, but anything is possible. The possibilities of lightness and love now outweigh the depths of darkness. I made a choice. A choice to stand up and be the beautiful, strong woman that I know I am. To tap into the resources that I have held within, that we all have within us. Some days are hard, and others are easy. I have the patience and kindness within me to accept that each day is a new one. The kindness and love we give ourselves is so precious and can make all of the difference in healing our scars and turning them into delicate reminders of who we can be and how strong we are. We can choose to be burdened by our scars, keeping them within and allowing them to burn holes deep into our sense of self worth. Or we can choose to be empowered by them, sharing openly with others to help and inspire. I have made my choice.

This scar will always be a part of who I am, and I am forever grateful as it makes me the beautiful woman that I am today. Giving me the capacity to love and laugh even deeper. Despite what lays ahead, I am discovering a sense of peace that what will be will be. My journey is not over, and I will not give up. Everything is exactly as it's meant to be in this moment.

To my fellow beautiful women, I say—with infinite love, peace, and wisdom, may each step we take be filled with compassion, gratitude, and grace. Thank you for listening. Thank you for sharing. Thank you for being you.

Chrissy's Story

Chrissy and I met at the yoga studio where we practice. I enjoyed her playful, intuitive way of teaching that made the suffering of the hot room laugh-out-loud fun. We have become great friends. We finish each other's sentences and have been on the same path of healing and being of service to the world. Something about Chrissy's energy helps others feel so much more alive and youthful. She has absolutely been made more beautiful by scars.

The Light of Dance and Breath

by Chrissy Beth

It began as a way to survive,
The control and restriction,
The self-punishment and starvation.
It was a way to stay small … on so many levels.
A secret and slow fading away.
At times, I truly thought it was a kind of
Freedom.
A freedom from everyone else's way.
A freedom from the right way, the only way.
But now I see it was actually the opposite,
Chains, a cage, clipping my wings so there could be
No chance of flight.
In the midst of the control, fear, and self-loathing,
I found movement with breath,
Strength in the slow, steady beat of my heart,
Beauty in my imperfectly perfect self.
I found yoga.
Thank you, Universe,
For sending me the light of dance
And breath …
For finding a way to connect my heart to my body
And my soul to my truth.
In yoga, I have become a woman who loves her own body,
The way it feels when I reach for the sky with my fingertips …
The way it feels as I hug the earth with my belly and heart.
I have become a woman who delights in the sensation of
Sweat slipping down my skin,
Heart pounding in my chest,
And the breath leading each moment.
Each breath is leading me to
A deeper connection to freedom.
If life before yoga was empty and starving,
It's now full of light, love, laughter, and play …
It's full of movement, growth, and an ever-expanding

Desire to leave the old layers behind.
As I move and flow, I release the chains
And unlock the cage around my heart.
In yoga, I am more connected to my
Playful spirit and the call of my wild, beautiful soul.
I no longer need the control of my anorexic mind.
The power her voice once held is gone, and instead
I hear music.
It's the song of freedom,
And I'm dancing,
Dancing,
Dancing
With gratitude for this life.

———

I spent over half my life trying to control my weight through starvation.

Having an eating disorder is very hard to describe to anyone who hasn't lived through it. It's like living in a dark cage. The part that is strange for people to understand on the outside is that the cage that you are choosing to lock yourself into when you hate your body feels "safe."

With an eating disorder, you create this safe cage for yourself, but the problem is that this cage is actually a really, really dark place, and it is the last place you should be, and yet it feels like the *only* place that actually is safe.

So to describe how it felt to live through an eating disorder to someone who has never experienced problems with body image, it sounds almost crazy. I know when I speak about it from a place of distance now, it does sound crazy, even to myself.

The thing is that it is not crazy to talk about how it feels when you are going through this battle. Eating disorders and body-image problems are so widespread that most people know someone or have multiple people in their lives that struggle with these problems. People die from eating disorders, and it is something that a lot of people don't feel they can talk about. When you do talk about it, out in society, there is almost a feeling that, "Well, you are *just* one of the club."

If you have an eating disorder, or you are struggling with your weight, or you are obsessed with exercising, it is seen as an accepted thing. Aren't all women supposed to hate their bodies? Haven't we all been conditioned to bond with other women over our distaste for our bodies?

It is a screwed-up thing that eating disorders are normal in our world because people can die from them. The amount of time and space in your mind and your heart that an eating disorder takes up is just not okay. It becomes your life.

Having an eating disorder is all-consuming. When you wake up, it is all you think about. Before you go to sleep, it is all you think about, and then you don't sleep very well because you are not healthy enough to get sleep. So you think about it at night while you are supposed to be sleeping.

I don't know when my eating disorder started. It's a hard thing to pinpoint exactly. I know it was early; I was very young when I first started believing that my body was a thing that I needed to be worried about. For some people, it starts gradually. Maybe they are carrying a little bit of extra weight and begin dieting, stop eating, and then it spirals out of control. Others do this with compulsive exercise.

For me it was more about two ideas—perfectionism and the idea of control. An eating disorder gave me something I could control, and it was a very private pleasure, this control. It was very secret. I was living in an environment where I didn't feel I had much control over my own choices, my own life, but this was one area I could control. A place of my own.

When I was in the thick of my eating disorder, the all-pervasive thought was private rebellion. I began to starve myself, and it made me feel in control.

There is a sad ideal in society that we are all pushed toward by those trying to sell us products, a fake ideal that we desperately try to live up to. This perfect image of what a woman is supposed to look like. As a young girl, I remember looking at magazines, at the models who were so thin and that defined what "beautiful" looked like.

Media uses celebrities with thin bodies to keep the pressure on—to keep us hopelessly reaching for that kind of beautiful. It's not obtainable because it is not real. Each photo that you see in a magazine advertisement has been retouched, shifted deliberately to create an image that no one can reach. It keeps us feeling like failures; it keeps us buying their stuff in the hope that maybe, just maybe we might be close to being worthwhile. It's all fake, smoke and mirrors, a dark magic show that is creating an epidemic of men and women starving themselves, throwing up meals, or exercising out of control.

I remember these patterns in myself. This desperate reach for the goal of being magazine worthy—reaching for the trophy, the finish line. The sad thing was it was always going to be out of reach for me and for anyone because this finish line *is not real*; it's all *fake*.

Along the way, in order to strive to perfection, I became anorexic. This gave me the idea that if I starved myself, then everything would be okay. If I just kept eating less and less, I would eventually get to the "happy" place. But it never comes, as it is an addictive disease. People used to say to me, "It's pretty simple. You just need to eat something. Why can't you just start eating again, you know, like a normal person? Why don't you go eat a cheese burger?" They meant well. It was just not that simple. I couldn't. I couldn't just eat more because then I would lose all control.

As a young girl, I remember a lot of voices talking about weight, a lot of female voices. These words are very powerful and leave an imprint, especially when you are small. I remember the voices around me very concerned and consumed with their image and the pressure of keeping their bodies under control. My anorexia comes with no blame, or an intention to put it on anyone around me, because I definitely took on this eating disorder on my own, with all my own responsibility, and I ran with it for years and years and years.

It felt very powerful to know I was doing something when all I could hear were other women around me saying hateful things about their own bodies. I learned early that I should have the same dark thoughts about myself. The voices I heard around me ignited a cruel voice inside—a voice that, when I think back to when I was in the deepest river of my disease, took me over. It was a loud voice. It created a lot of guilt and fear. I gave over all my power to the voice of my eating disorder, and I lived with that voice for years.

I can't say exactly when it stopped. I don't have those voices anymore. It was a slow, gradual process toward healing. Many people think that an eating disorder is for life. It is just not true. You don't have to keep the voice. You don't have to live in the cage. You can be free. True freedom is living a beautiful life away from a crazy, mean, dark, and destructive voice in your head. It tells you that you are not worthy and that you do not deserve real unconditional love within, and you do. You really do deserve all that—and more.

Eating disorders can run through families. I remember my grandmother was always concerned about what she ate, right up to her death. It's very sad. She was a beautiful woman to waste so much time thinking about that. The concept of being beautiful—whatever beautiful was meant to be—was introduced to me at a very young age. I feel very passionately that we need to be so very careful of our words, not just around young people but also around all people.

Watch your words because they shape children's perception of their own bodies. Your daughters, your sons, your niece, your younger sister. People that come to you for any sort of advice or guidance, they are listening, so be aware of the words that you use around the people that you love. If your words are body-image negative, if they are disempowering about you or other people's bodies in any way, this is something that others tune into, especially younger people.

We need to stop attacking our bodies. We need to have more compassion, use more compassionate, loving words toward ourselves. Gentler words, so we can pass that on to our children, to the younger generation, to friends, but in general just to the people around you.

I was raised in a very religious home and went to church several times a week. My dad was a leader in the church, and it felt like people were always watching. I could feel it. I leaned toward that leadership energy myself, leading Bible study groups, singing, guiding others. This was a big part of my life. In any sort of organized community or religion, there can be an element of being controlled, of being told right from wrong, good from bad, a way to live and a way not to live.

Some of the things that I struggled with—the control, the weight of religion—led me to want to find some control of my own. Any community has its negatives and positives. As I got older, I struggled with not having enough freedom. For me, the eating disorder, in a really twisted way, gave me freedom. Freedom from the boxes I was expected to live in.

For women and young girls, we are raised to grow up and be "pretty." When you are a girl, you wear pink, put on the tutu, and you are a princess. For me, there was this pressure to be a good girl, a good Christian girl. I was really good at that. I didn't cause any trouble. I was a leader, a role model for others. I didn't feel I had the freedom to think my own thoughts. I didn't feel free to explore life outside of those looped boxes, and so I do believe that for me my eating disorder created some sort of personal place I could kick at the boxes surrounding me. It gave me some wings to fly, but I was in a cage. I couldn't fly anywhere.

As we grow from a young girl into a woman and our bodies are changing, there is sometimes this pressure to stay this pretty, sweet little girl. But everything changes; hormones kick in, and the sweet little girl is meant to leave at that point and be replaced with a powerful woman. The way that you think starts to change. You become a sexual being, which is very natural as a human but not so natural for me when I was living under the control of a church that had a lot of distaste over sex. Sex was looked at as a negative thing. I could hear around me a lot of control language and judgment around sex in general and in particular having sex.

As I left the pretty, young little girl stage and started to mature into being a woman, a way I could control this powerful, growing energy within me, an energy that I had been taught was bad, was to try to stop growing up. A lot of girls enter anorexia around puberty. A consequence of extreme starvation is that your body thinks that you have been plunged into famine, so it shuts down your periods. It is trying to keep you safe, as famine is not the ideal environment to grow a human being. That happened to me. I didn't get my period for a long time.

It's a strange thought process. As my body was changing before my eyes, I felt the need to dial that down, as I would be more loveable to the people around me if I stayed a sweet and innocent young girl. An eating disorder dials your big energy down and makes you numb. Your sexual power is turned off. Your ability to create life is turned off. This is a powerful price to take away your gift as a woman to connect as a fully expressed human being, a creative force of nature. To stay small, young, sweet, and innocent was part of the puzzle of anorexia for me. It turned down my laugh, my song, and my joy. I felt the need to stay small.

With an eating disorder, you *contain* yourself, and that's disturbing. For women, there is a lot of that in our society. When a woman becomes powerful, loud, or starts to speak her truth as a leader, if she exudes a sexual, creative energy, out come the trolls.

"Quick! Shut her down! That woman is way too much. What's her problem?"

I think our world is changing, and it is shifting to allow women to be more of themselves, but it is still not enough. Any time someone has an eating disorder, they are looking for a way to be smaller—no matter what type of eating disorder you have.

Another thing I want to share is the secretive element of having an eating disorder. A lot of the time, you don't even know that the person around you has this disease. It is so well hidden. Having an eating disorder doesn't necessarily mean that you look emaciated. Sometimes you look like everyone else, and others have no idea that you are deeply sick inside, consumed with every thought around food or exercise and how to manage it. It is a myth that you have to look like you are starving to have an eating disorder. I was very good at being sneaky and had a whole plethora of creative ways to get out of eating, to keep my cage securely locked.

In that secrecy, you create a safe little world, and you definitely don't want someone to take that away from you, so you fight to keep it. I certainly wasn't going to talk to anyone about my private pain, to let anyone know that I was controlling every morsel that went into my mouth. It was a personal high—all of my own. When people started to notice and question my behavior, I was very good at making up reasons. This secrecy is part of the consuming, addictive nature of control in this disease.

The plotting and the planning take up a lot of your life. You stop living your life. You think that this is living, this wonderful fantasy world where you get to call all the shots, but you are not living, just existing, addicted to the buzz of constant anxiety and control. It was not living for me, living in this lonely cage. I just existed, and we are here for so much more than that.

The eating disorder voice and the cage left me through the healing power of my yoga practice. It is the reason why I am recovered and stay in my freedom. Ironically, when I first found yoga, I chose a style of yoga that was very controlled. Bikram yoga is taught in a hot room, it is highly structured, and you follow a specific set of postures that don't change. The yoga took the control from inside me and gave me the outlet to move, free, and love my body. Yoga helps me stay connected and in touch with my true voice, the kind, genuine one, and away from the ugly eating disorder voice. I love music and bring the energy of playfulness into the room when I teach. Yoga heals the body from the inside out, and it healed me.

I have found a few different teachers that have inspired me into a freer flow in my yoga practice and as a yoga teacher. I still love practicing and teaching in a hot room, but there is more playfulness in my yoga today. The practice keeps me connected to my heart compass, my intuition, and my true voice. I believe this is what happens for many people with the breath, movement, and meditation of yoga. It is a powerful healing tool that has balanced me. I am forever grateful for my practice, and it will always be a part of my life because it keeps me healthy, it keeps me happy, joyful, and playful, and it's a continuous forever journey that never ends, always going deeper into my heart and my true path.

So, when someone asks me, "When did you recover from your eating disorder? When did it stop?" I have no idea. I just know that it's gone and it's not coming back, as through my practice I have created a different kind of healthy safety net. A safety net that holds me. It takes me along some twisting, wild roads at times, roads that need to be seen, roads that I have hidden from myself and need to let go of—and they do go. I can say that I am the most free I have ever felt. I am not saying that I don't have any fear; I do, I'm human, but not the kind of fear I used to have in the midst of the eating disorder because that's crippling. It takes over your life.

My life is so much more about love now. Loving myself, loving the people around me, even the ones that are harder to love, those I don't know that well. I now allow my voice—my sound—my singing. I trust what comes out of my mouth without second-guessing these days.

There was a time when I thought it was best to tuck my wings away. It felt safe, less chance of falling, not as risky. Without my wings, I could stay small. I wasn't as visible or expansive. But at some point your wings need to open up, spread, and feel the wide-open space. It gets exhausting trying to hide them for too long. On my twenty-fifth birthday, without telling a soul, at a time when I felt trapped in a life of control, I drove myself to the nearest tattoo parlor and had my wings permanently painted on my back.

We are not born to be perfect. We are each one of us imperfectly perfect. Your vulnerability is a thing of beauty. It can be scary to show people the parts of us that are a bit rough, unpolished, the messier bits. But those are the best bits. Those pieces are what make you the authentically amazing person you are right now. Not the person your parents want you to be, or your partner or the people in your community. Not the person you thought you'd be by now. None of that is real. It's who you are right now, today, with your (cracked) heart on your sleeve and your eyes shining from the knowledge that this is when the magic happens. When you set your fear aside and let the walls come down. Your vulnerability is a thing of beauty.

Wild, open, free … when we are all of these things, we are connected to our true authentic self. Children know this; they aren't afraid to express their joy, fear, or pain. As we get older, we put up fences, accumulate locks, and do our best to hide behind society-approved masks. Your wild self is still there, waiting for you to sever the cord from these things in your life that aren't real, the plastic stage you've created. This is the real deal, this life. So screw the plastic stage and people and things! Be wild, be real; it might get messy but better messy than numb. Wild feels good. Wild is beautiful. The world needs more of your wild.

My scars have taught me to follow my own heart compass. Call it gut, intuition, your true voice, soul … it boils down to the place inside of you that knows your path. The heart compass guides you on those twisty, crazy roads of life. My heart compass will sometimes ask me to take risks, to venture off of the safer path and find the one that's not yet been explored. This is all part of our adventure, the soft and hard, the joy and pain. It's pretty epic to tune into your own beat, your heartbeat, and follow the rhythm … to follow your own heart.

Love is my home.

Yuki He Photography

Joyce's Story

I was drawn into Joyce's art studio and felt the powerful light in her work. She is extraordinarily talented and creates from her soul. She collects driftwood by the ocean, and the wood calls to her to create art from the inside out. I have several of her driftwood angels and canvases. Originally from Holland, Joyce had been living in Christchurch when the earthquake struck and destroyed much of the inner city. Left it broken rubble. She was a calm light in the storm of that time for many, and this artwork and poem is inspired by that experience.

Loudly boasted for their size.
Silently suffered for Their depth.
Superficially showing on skin
Or hurting deeply within.

For all these are true
Somehow …
They make us stronger
And more beautiful too,

These scars …

Image of an original painting by
by Joyce van der Lely called
Beautiful by Scars

Corrine's Story

Corrine has a passion for educating women about purchasing products from sustainable sources. She helps women feel seen and even convinced me to be a runway model for one of her fashion shows. It felt empowering to do that at forty-five years old! Corrine once told me she was shy. I laughed, as I think she is one of the strongest and most insightful women I have ever met!

"We are what we pretend to be, so we must be careful
what we pretend to be."

—Kurt Vonnegut, *Mother Night*

always knew I would like to be a mother someday. Once I was done with travelling, had established a career, and was committed in a relationship. I knew that once I was settled and happy in who I was as a person, I would be ready to be responsible for someone else.

Pregnancy was easy for me, but once my son was born, I was overwhelmed by sleep deprivation and the noise of a constantly crying child.

I was not prepared for the onslaught of emotional stress, pressure, and exhaustion, of being a mother and wife combined, plus the weight of expectation, of watching my every move, as I remained stuck inside the house for the traditional Chinese thirty days of confinement.

In my culture, all mothers have a confinement period of four weeks, where we are housebound and cared for by our mother, mother-in-law, or a special confinement support woman. The Chinese believe that the mother's body needs time to repair and heal from childbirth. The belief is that outside air, cold water, and germs are dangerous in those early days.

The confinement helper is supposed to take care of everything in the household, including cooking all the meals for the new mother and helping with the baby so that the mother can focus solely on resting and healing her body.

My mum and dad moved in with us for four months to keep me company and offer this confinement help. With their experience and pure joy of being grandparents, they took it in their stride to take over the house and help care for their grandson.

Both my husband and I were complete beginners in parenting, and like other young parents, we had the intention of wanting to experience learning how to care for our child ourselves. This wasn't possible during the time of confinement.

It was hard to feel sure and capable in these early days, and for my partner, the intensity of being watched and getting it right as a young dad made him fearful of holding such a fragile baby. Made it hard for him.

For me, the emotions that were rampant, and the number of low moments within were overwhelming. No one tells you the truth about how awful you can feel and how incredibly hard it actually is to be a parent. How much of a toll it takes on the relationship between you and your partner and how much energy it takes to deal with your issues, let alone helping your partner cope with the dramatic change in both your lives. Add into that soup of emotions the tension and bubbling conflicts happening in your house when you have extra family members living together, you lose connection with your center.

Expectation is a big word.

How often do partners discuss their expectations of each other before they get married or have a baby?

We had a weekend of pre-marriage education, a counseling session before we married at the local Catholic church. There was no in-depth discussion about parenting or what we expected from each other when raising a child. We didn't talk about the way we were each brought up or how we were going to help each other and make time for each other as a couple.

Eight years down the road, I realized that my husband and I were brought up very differently from each other, had completely different understandings of how a mother or a father should be, and our opposing ways of thinking led to a multitude of misunderstandings and problems.

I remember when I first told my husband about the emotional stress, the turmoil that I was feeling inside as a new mum. He offered to take me for a five-day holiday with him to Hong Kong, and I tried to explain how I could not just leave our two-month-old son and go with him. He said to me, "You have gone completely mad. Do you want us to separate?" He was frustrated and obviously trying to find a way back to an "us" outside the constant demands of the baby and family in the house. At that time though, he didn't have the words to know what to say.

I remember asking him if he could help me with some of the night feeds and settling our son and him saying, "I have to work and wake up at 5:00 a.m., so I can't be too tired." At that time, I felt like it was a slap in the face. I felt alone in our relationship. I guess I was looking for the Johnson and Johnson advertisement—the loving mum and dad adoringly taking care of their child together.

I think that men also face powerful challenges when becoming a father for the first time, and when their partner's time, attention, and energy are taken away from them, they feel that's not what they bargained for. Add in family pressure, they feel shoved out. They feel left behind.

Expectation energy at this time was intense. It was extraordinarily exhausting to maintain a front that I was happy and coping in front of others. I could smile and be chatty when I had visitors, but after they left, I felt empty and went back to feeling very low, negative, wanting to run away as far as I could … forever.

Even with the amount of hands-on support I was getting, I began feeling super anxious, doubting my mothering abilities. Unexpressed resentment toward my partner for not spending more time with me and with the baby began to creep in, and I began to feel numb, alone, and empty on the inside. When the baby cried, I felt only exhaustion rather than warmth. I couldn't eat, couldn't sleep, and couldn't get motivated to do anything other than just laying in bed dwelling on negativity.

Two weeks later on the point of collapse, my milk just stopped. My mother stepped in and took over care of my son. I drove myself to the local GP and left with a diagnosis of postnatal anxiety and a script for strong antidepressants. I had to make a decision then and there to give up all hope for breastfeeding before the situation worsened. I spoke to my partner, who had since our last big episode talked to a friend who explained the symptoms and severity of postnatal depression to him. He understood, changed his attitude, and gave me his full and loving support.

Explaining how I was really feeling to extended family was another thing altogether. In the world of Chinese culture, no one talks about postnatal issues. You are meant to just toughen up and carry on. Put on the smiling face. I chose not to speak to family about what was happening to me.

After taking the first dose of antianxiety medication and a sleeping pill, I slept for two whole days straight and woke up a new woman, emotionally and physically stronger.

My son had colic, eczema, and food allergies. Things got harder with him, not easier, but I was able to cope. I got great advice and support to help manage his condition, and then we relocated to a new city.

Starting a new chapter together and getting away on our own was the best way for me to face up to my own issues and find a way to move forward as our own little family. Being grounded and knowing I could be self-sufficient as a mother was an amazing turning point. Bonding as an immediate family made my soul happy. Now I didn't feel like wanting to run. Now I knew I could do this.

With a toddler newly walking, we started life in a new city. My parents came for the first three weeks and then left us to explore life, explore the city with my little boy, doing activities with him while my husband was at work. The three of us had all the time in the world to bond and do our own thing without the obligation of family and friends. I joined a mums' group—women who to this day are my best friends here.

I had the opportunity during this time to deeply figure out what I wanted to do going forward. I felt totally refreshed, energized, and motivated to do something to support my family, something that I could be passionate about. I set up a small business from home, something that meant a lot to me, creating ethical fashion and accessories. Helping women access these products that were not made by cheap underpaid labor but by people who were valued for their time and rewarded ethically meant a lot to me. My business, Lacorvin, became all about supporting local artisans who sourced high-quality raw materials using sustainable methods and as a result creating handcrafted accessories that would last a lifetime.

My brand value and mission was to make a difference in the world one accessory at a time. I knew that my business would help many women artisans have a better quality life. Having a business was a huge turning point on the road to conquering postnatal anxiety and depression, an achievement made on hard work and self-belief. It gave me the flexibility to work around the needs of my small child and freedom to do something that mattered.

My experience with postnatal depression taught me to speak up and organize family or friends to support and help me when I needed it, especially when organizing big retail events. I did not try to be Superwoman or put on the face anymore and pretend to cope. I learned to let go of any anxiety I once had about asking for help.

Connecting with other women entrepreneurs has been amazing. The willingness to share raw stories, collaborate, support each other, laugh, and boost each other up through all the down moments and scary challenges faced in small-business survival has been one of the most humbling and beautiful experiences I have had. Without my scar of postnatal anxiety, I don't know if I would have learned to be so raw and real with others, or so brave in myself.

For other women going through emotional distress, postnatal anxiety, or depression, my advice is to gently nurture you. Speak up. Speak your truth. Be brave and find your purpose, something that brings you joy. It doesn't matter what it is—just find it. Finding your balance and the support you need to get through can only happen if you make it a priority to find a way back to loving yourself on the inside. Most importantly, being a mother doesn't mean you have to give up on you, on what you love, on what makes you *you*. You can be a mum *and* be you too!

As a new mum, our family members (especially in Chinese families!) love to give you advice. When you are exhausted and unsure of how to be a parent, this can feel overwhelming. There is something vital and special about having the time to build a bond with your own child, making mistakes yourself and then learning how to mother. What I now know is that it is okay to say no to people and their parenting advice. Let them know that you appreciate them, but to grow into being a mum, you have to be allowed to experience parenting for yourself, do a lot of things wrong in order to learn how to do them right—not perfect but right enough for you and those you love.

I have learned that it is okay as a new mother to cut yourself some slack. It's okay to feel fat, sad, irritated, and frustrated, to feel like you are failing. There is no such thing as perfect parenting, and learning about being a parent is a constant. Juggling demands every day is a constant. Lack of sleep is hard. Be patient with yourself and with your partner. Make time to giggle and to cuddle. Make time not to be so serious. Forgive yourself and those you love when you say things you didn't really mean—when you are both tired and overwhelmed.

It's a big job being a parent. If you can forgive each other when you make mistakes, you can learn together and not build resentment but instead a real and genuine journey that knits together the hard and the beautiful times and makes a deeper and ultimately more loving relationship—because it is real.

You can be a kickass mother, partner, friend, and creator of your own destiny. Women are a powerful creative force.

Women are the givers and creators of life, and we can achieve anything.

Corrine

Sandra's Story

Sandra and I shared a four-hour taxi ride through the winding hills of Bali in late 2015. We were both travelling to a healing retreat and immediately bonded. Our stories were very similar as healers. We had also both recovered from debilitating disease to find life, health, and joy once more. Sandra is a veterinarian who lives in China. She has the best smile and a heart that would hold the whole world.

The Long Road Home

All my life I chased for love.
I bent, I bowed, I scraped for love.
To be valued, wanted, seen and heard,
So desperate I was, I pledged to learn,
To please, to serve, to be a good girl,
To learn the "right way" to be a woman in a man's world.
But they could not see me, or if so, not for long,
Because the way I looked and acted was oh so wrong.
Too sensual, too voluptuous, too much of a threat,
So they'd lie and cheat, take all they could get.
Or hate me instantly for what I could not help but be,
        Instead of seeing all the beauty and love right there inside of me.
        In this way, I learned to hate myself,
To punish, to judge, to hide up on a shelf.
Trying to bend and fold so I'd fit in their box,
Till the whole damn act became a big box of rocks.
What was to become of me? What was in store?
So scared I was when I couldn't pretend anymore.
If I couldn't convince them I was worthy before,
What on earth was I here for?
And now here I am, having found my tribe,
Scattered across the globe both far and wide.
Having learned the most incredible lesson of all,
That the goddess lives inside me and will never let me fall.
She brought me here this time around,
To stamp, to shout, to shake the ground!
To rock the world with my love and passion,
To serve the world in my own unique fashion.
Spreading light and love across the globe,
To shine a light so others know which way to go.
A path so hard for many to find, because it's not for sale
And doesn't live in their mind.
Instead the way lives within themselves,
With all those beautiful souls, hidden up on those shelves.
So I go forth now to ring the bell,

To help stop other people from living in hell.
Simply by being myself, being true to the real me,
And bravely letting the whole world see
That I am a goddess, fierce and true,
Exactly like the one inside every one of you!

Namaste.

Lucia's Story

Lucia's story was meant to be in the book. I believe that the women who will share their stories will turn up when they are meant to, and it will be beyond obvious. Seeing Lucia's Facebook post about gratitude and reflection on her five-year anniversary of scars led me to contact her. I'm glad I reached out and even more glad that she offered to stop and write down her brave story instead of painting the hallway!

$\mathcal{F}$irstly I would like to apologize. I am not much of a writer. This story is going to be the rambling thoughts running through my head, just an honest account of my personal experience of living with scars.

Today I posted up a YouTube clip, uploaded five years ago, of my husband and I being surprised by our friends with a fun run on the day that was meant to be our wedding day. It was not to be, as we were involved in a serious car accident.

I wrote: "Taking the time today to reflect and feel blessed. Five years ago today, Gaz and I were ready to marry. A car accident stopped that, but the incredible love and support from our friends made the day every bit as special. Love to you all."

Within the hour of the post, I was down at the park playing with my toddler, and I received a message from Veronica. She was publishing a book titled *Made Beautiful by Scars* and asked me if I would I be interested in telling my story.

My instant thought was, *why would anyone outside of my friends and family be interested in my story?*

And besides that, I am so busy at the moment with my little one, work, housework, and I am still only halfway through painting the hallway ...

No, I will message her back and say, I can't.

And as soon as I thought that, I stopped myself. If I had learned anything since the accident, it was that:

You never know what life holds.

Take great opportunities.

Get over yourself.

Who cares if the washing gets done? I won't remember *that* next week, let alone a year from now!

So ...

Why not take a moment to sit down, type, and, as I said in my Facebook post, "reflect"?

So home I went from the park to put Otto down for his afternoon nap and began my ramble ...

What happened?

On December the 27, 2010, at around 5:00 p.m., I was travelling south out of Napier on State Highway 2 in the middle of the North Island of New Zealand. My mother-in-law was driving, my father-in-law was the front passenger, my sister-in-law was to my right, and Gaz, my partner, was to my left. I was center back.

I was dozing off as we came up around a bend. A scream and Gaz throwing his arm across me startled me awake to glimpse a car coming head-on at us.

The rest is just like a crash in the movies, everything went in slow motion. I saw the windscreen shatter, my mother-in-law's thigh moving in midair. My brain screamed, "This is going to be really bad!"

Then in a fragment of a second, it was over.

Then the screams, the howls, the pungent smell of mangled cars, and of course the pain all hit.

Everyone jumped out of the car, except me. I was slumped down in the foot well and couldn't move. I wiggled my fingers and toes as much as I could. In my mind, I could remember my mother's words, "If you can move those, it's a good start."

The car was smoking, and I became panicked, begging to get out, even though I knew my neck was bad. My father-in-law, who had taken a hit to the head but was mobile, scooped me out. Thankfully he is a big, strong farmer, so he did this with not too much trouble. I was laid out flat next to the car.

What about Gaz? Where is he?

I couldn't see him. I was told he had collapsed on the other side of the vehicle.

Screaming, shouting, anger, confusion, continued for twenty minutes until the police and ambulances arrived. Until that time, civilians that narrowly missed being involved in the three-car and truck pile up, of which twelve people where involved, helped to get things under control.

A retired paramedic was in the car that followed us; he was a guardian angel, keeping things together and constantly checking on us until help arrived.

Gaz was taken away by emergency helicopter, due to internal bleeding; he lost two liters of blood and was lucky to survive his internal injuries.

Out of twelve people involved in the crash, there were several shattered bones and a concussion, but Gaz and I were the only ones that ended up in intensive care.

Gaz's injuries were far worse than mine, but that is a whole other story. My injuries included a ruptured bowel, hernias that were treated in emergency surgery, and neck trauma. I was placed in a neck brace upon arrival of the ambulance.

After a week of intensive care, I was put in a standard ward. Thinking I was on the up and up, I started to get out of bed and take a few steps—then began to lose the feeling in the tops of my fingers on my right hand.

I didn't think much of it, but as it got worse, I mentioned it and was then sent off for more X-rays. This revealed that I had a fractured C6 and C7 and needed to be put into a stable position as soon as possible.

Things really took a turn for the worse at this point; the doctors talked me through the process of having to be put into traction.

This involved going into surgery awake, using a local anesthetic while they drilled holes into my skull above my eyebrows and behind my ears. My bone would anchor the bolts that would hold the metal halo that would go around my head. Then a wire with weights would be added in fifteen-gram increments, until my spine was guided into the correct position.

It was necessary to be awake throughout the procedure so that I could tell them what I was feeling and if I was losing any sensation in my body.

Once this was completed, I was wheeled back to my ward, flat on my back, unable to move.

I was desperate to know how long I would be like this.

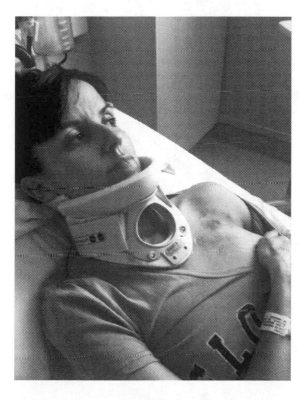

The nurses said it could be days, weeks. I was terrified; I just didn't think I would have the mental strength.

I couldn't do a thing, I was a prisoner in bed, and I ate, slept, took my pain relief, and went to the toilet, flat on my back.

Four nurses would come to turn and clean me twice a day so that I wouldn't get bedsores. They would have to line up next to my bedside and count down, turning my whole body simultaneously, as the weights that hung from my halo down the back of the bed would click along the wire, and back again when they rolled me back.

I lay staring at the ceiling. People's faces would pop in and out of my sight above me, but I just wanted to be left alone.

Depression started to creep in. All I wanted was to know what was happening, something solid that I could work toward.

Thankfully, after three days, I got a huge break. My X-rays had been sent to a specialist in Auckland, and I was to be airlifted the next day, transferred for spinal surgery.

I was so relived. The following morning, a team came to body wrap me in a type of beanbag that has the air sucked out of it, so that I was held firmly inside it, sweating and unable to move and on my way.

Dr. Angus Don popped his head into my sight, with his scrubs cap on, introducing himself, then asked for a spanner so that he could kindly get the "terrible thing" off my head.

Taking full control of the situation, he reassured me he would see me in theater in a couple of hours, after my MRI.

They say patients fall in love with their doctors, and I totally get it now. Wow—talk about my hero!

I had bone taken from my hip and screwed into my spine. After surgery, I was sitting up in a neck brace, back on track. It all went well, and I would make a full recovery.

I was housebound, recovering for six weeks. I was very weak, on lots of pain relief. My mum came to take care of me. Cooking, cleaning, she was amazing. A nurse came every other day to change all my dressings.

Gaz came home a few weeks after me but unfortunately ended up back in hospital again, due to complications.

Looking back now, it was so tough worrying about Gaz, going to the hospital, dithering along in my neck brace to be at his side. But really the entire time, both Gaz and I have only felt lucky. Hugely lucky to be alive, to get well again, to have the family and friends that we do, who looked after us beyond what we could ever have imagined.

People would always say to me, "You're so strong. You're amazing how you have handled what happened." But I can honestly say I'm not at all. When something like this happens to you, it's just getting through one day at a time.

You are forced to slow down, go inside yourself, be motivated to find health. I had such a thirst to be well, get my life back, and thankfully I was blessed enough to have that happen.

Gaz and I went on to marry in May 2011. We were still fragile and underweight, and we laugh at the photos now, at just how thin we both were.

Tears flowed freely on our wedding day, but not a drop from Gaz's eyes and mine; we just smiled and felt so happy to have made it.

In 2014, we welcomed our little boy, Otto, another blessing, as even though one of my ovaries was damaged and I had poor circulation in my uterus from scar tissue, after much trying and the help of an incredible acupuncturist, we have so much joy in our lives.

Live, life, love.

It's not what happens to you in life; it's how you handle it that matters!

Love,

Lucia

Photography by Carolyn Haslett

119

Sara's Story

Sara heard about Made Beautiful by Scars from her partner, Paige, who is a friend of mine. He told me that Sara's story needed to be in the book. I believed him. Sara has a great story.

Photography by Lauren Mead

J was one of those people who would tell others, "I don't have an addictive personality. I'll be all right." I don't know who I was trying to convince more—them or me.

I was always convinced that all the bad stuff having to do with drugs happened to someone else, happened to the junkie that lived in west Melbourne, happened to the people that couldn't control themselves. How wrong I was. Cocaine was my Achilles' heel. It took me on some fascinating journeys where I would play in the fifth dimension and not want to return. And on one particular afternoon, I almost didn't.

It was an accident. I'd been up for several days (I don't remember how long), and I booted too much—like *way* too much—in one hit. It left me frothing on the floor, unconscious, requiring reviving. They very nearly lost me. The drug had me so ferociously that as soon as I got out of hospital after my overdose, the first thing I went and did was use again. I had no awareness around what a problem it had become and what damage it was doing to not only my physiology and my mental state but also my psyche.

It tore my soul into millions of pieces.

I thought I would never be able to pick myself up and put myself back together, and no one could save me but me. There came a time when the love for the drug wore off; the come down just wasn't worth it anymore, and it ran its course.

I survived. Just.

I got therapy, I got clean with the support of my husband, and I learned to never underestimate the power drugs can have over you when you're vulnerable or lacking on the inside. I learned that I already had what I thought drugs were giving me. I just needed to love me.

Just as I was.

Just as I am.

Don't get me wrong. I still have my moments that pull me toward wishing for escape—that piece of the brain that seeks newness, powerful excitement. But I know myself well enough to know I'm not bulletproof. I'm a work in progress. I'm no genius by any stretch, although I have enough awareness to see patterns forming (time off work, negative mind chatter, bad moods, cravings, relationship breakdowns) to know there's a problem. And I'm much better equipped to manage myself these days.

Step number one: love myself.

Check!

I have all the tools available at my disposal if I just remember to stop, pause, and stay present in this moment. Having a meditation practice helps enormously, and I feel sometimes that if I hadn't located my spiritual bent, I'd be back down the deep, dark rabbit hole again. I'm so grateful to have had all those crazy, intense, reckless, life-changing experiences. But what I'm even more grateful for now is that I have compassion for the little girl who was crying out on the inside trying to tear her way out, trying to be heard, trying to be seen.

She just wanted to be seen.

Well I see, you little one, and I got you.

Tanya's Story

Tanya emits such power and vitality from her body. In her yoga teaching, she helps everyone in the room, irrespective of age or flexibility, feel able to go that one step further, be brave, feel the body, and move with strength. Her early life scars taught her that gift—the gift of the body and how to inspire others to find joy in theirs.

I was born and raised in Johannesburg, South Africa. I am the middle child, and I have two beautiful sisters. Belinda is my older sister, and Louise (Lulu as she is fondly known) is my younger sister.

I was three years old when Lulu was born. Mum tells us that Lulu was sickly from the start. She was born without a thyroid, and back in those days, this wasn't something that was tested for at birth, so it was only discovered when she was three months old. The thyroid gland is needed for everything to grow in the body, both mentally and physically. This was a huge shock to my parents, as it meant she had an incurable disease and that she would always struggle.

Lulu had her first eye operation at nine months, and she wore glasses from the age of two. She could do a forward roll without them falling off, and it was very cute to see. Lulu went to a school for children with special needs. She loved going to school.

Around the age of three, Lulu started to get a series of colds and flus and complained of terrible pains in her legs. It got so bad that she spent three months in the hospital while they did a million tests, and finally she was diagnosed with rheumatoid arthritis, a very painful disease in the joints. Our family tried to carry on as normal, but she was always in a lot of pain, and we could feel that.

We went on holiday to Cape Town, and I clearly remember Lulu not being well the whole time. Even with this in the background, it was a special holiday as a family. I guess we were trying our best to be normal and have a normal holiday. We came back to Johannesburg and had to rush her straight to the hospital. After many more tests, we were told she had neuroblastoma. Cancer. She had a growth on her adrenal gland, and it was spreading into her brain. Devastating is not even close to how it felt to hear this news.

The cancer had spread extensively, but they started treatment the next day. Lulu had a series of chemo treatments, and she lost her hair. She had a Hickman line put in. It is a plastic line inserted into the chest under the skin and then up into the jugular vein and straight into the heart. This line is a life send and allows for blood transfusions, drug administration, and chemotherapy to be administered without having to always look for a vein and jabbing needles into little people. I have in my mind a beautiful memory of Lulu standing on the steps of our pool, white as snow from literally living in the hospital, with that great big bandage on her where the line went in.

My mother and father were absolute saints through this all. Mom would work all day and then go to stay with Lulu in the hospital through the night, leaving at 4:00 a.m. to come home and sort out the rest of us. If I think of myself doing that now, and I could not fathom it. I know I would if I had to, but my mom went through very tough years, and it took its toll on her body.

During these years, my sister and I were always staying with some friend or relative, so from a very young age, I had to learn how to be self-sufficient. This had a big impact on the kind of person I have become. I didn't really see this at the time, and I was sometimes angry that my parents weren't around, but I now know that they really had no choice and they were doing the best they could in the situation. It was pretty tough, but I'm a very resilient person.

Lulu was given so many different types of treatments. Everything was tried over the two years, but eventually it was decided that we would stop, as nothing was working and she was just in agony from it all. Belinda and I were taken to see her one night; I knew something was wrong, as there were many family members around. I was staying at my aunt's house and remember so very clearly her waking me early the next morning to tell me that Lulu was gone.

Lulu lost the battle to cancer at the age of five and a half. I was eight, and my sister Belinda was twelve. At the time, I suppose I was more confused than anything else. I knew that she had gone to go live with the Lord, but it was only as I got older that I started to go through the process of how it feels to lose someone so close to you at such a young age. Belinda, being older, struggled straight away in her grieving. She is a quieter person by nature, so she internalized it.

My parents were completely heartbroken but had to carry on, as they had two other children to look after. As a family, we always talk about Lulu and how special she was and the funny things she did. We have kept her memory alive. We still cry, a lot.

As I grew older and started to become more emotionally aware, I started to explore in myself what it meant to me to lose a sister. It's hard. It sucks big time. You think about it all the time, and everything I did, I would think of Lulu. But I'm a naturally upbeat kind of person, so I decided to live my life in memory of my sister. Be strong for her.

I decided to live my life to the fullest. Knowing that she couldn't do all the amazing things—like have your first kiss, go to your first dance, get married, climb a mountain, travel the world—I would do these things and think that I was doing it for Lulu, who would never get to experience this amazing life. This was my way of making sense of it all and turning the situation around. I am a much stronger person from this. Losing a sister changes you. I'm pretty tough because of it.

As a result, I became very aware of my health from a young age. I wanted a strong body and have always taken care of myself, doing lots of sports and eating well. Having this awareness of one's physicality, I love to teach others how to honor their bodies and how lucky we are to be alive and have a body that works. I have brought this into my teaching of yoga, and I get great pleasure in guiding people in their yoga practice and seeing them evolve in themselves both physically and emotionally.

When I became a mother and had my own children, I felt the pain of Lulu anew and in a different way. I look at my two boys and try to imagine what it must be like to lose one of them. I break down right then and there because I would just die if that had to happen to me, and this has given me a new respect for my parents and what they went through. I have always been very close to my parents, but we are even more so now that I have kids.

You never forget. The pain never goes away. You just learn how to be strong and keep on living.

My gift for Lulu has been to be strong in my body and teach others to be the same. It was hard as a child being around chronic illness and not having any tools to heal it, to take away the pain from my sister and from my parents. I know that keeping your body strong through good food and healing yoga helps, and I will keep teaching that work so I can see others in my classes get stronger, healthier, and more vibrant in their own lives, for themselves and for their families.

This is part of a poem by my mom, Marian. This was placed in the warm heart of our home …

In Loving Memory of Louise

Beautiful memories,
Tears unseen,
Wishing your absence
Was just a dream.
We miss you, Lulu
And always will.
You left a place
No one can fill.
Memories never fade;
They just grow deep
Of one we loved
And could not keep.
"I'm just a little girl
Who didn't quite make it there.
I've gone to be with Jesus,
And I'm waiting for you there.
So, don't worry about me, Mommy.
I'm of God's lambs most blessed.
I would have liked to stay with you,
But the Shepherd knows what's best.
Thank you for the life you gave me.
It was brief, but don't complain.
I've gained all heaven's glory,
Suffered none of earthlings' pain.
Thank you for the name you gave me.
I would have liked to bring it fame.
So, my sweet Mommy,
Dry the tears and ease the gloom.
Keep on living."

Chantelle's Story

I trust intuition, especially when it smacks you in the face. I had been drawn to understanding the power of tantric bodywork, and when I saw a retreat that Chantelle was facilitating, I knew I just had to be there. I learned a great deal at this workshop in Bali, about myself, about how we distance ourselves from the pain and the beauty of our body and tell ourselves so many stories that keep us from our inner radiance and sensuality. Chantelle is a powerful being, self-reflective, passionate, and intelligent. She owns her scars like a lioness—beautifully, fierce, with her head held high ...

$\mathcal{T}$o the outside world, I was living the dream—a successful businesswoman with a six-figure income, three degrees behind me, two beautiful children, a loving husband, a big house by the beach, regular exotic travels, and lots of spiritual glam.

Then I got the news that I had cervical cancer.

Fortunately, I had been trained from a very early age from my father to see life as a dream of sorts. In other words, everything that happens is for a reason and is simply the will of God or Spirit.

What we are here to practice is love, kindness, compassion, and forgiveness, even with the most challenging of people.

Growing up, I had to be self-sufficient and self-nurturing. There was a gift in this; from a very early age, I learned to put my "stuff" aside and show up in love. I still hear my father's words now: "Focus on what you can give, not on what you can get."

He also helped me to see the bigger picture. "How can you come from love? How can you grow from this?"

I knew there was a message in this news about my cervix. I approached it the same way I approached all challenges at the time—with my mind. This, however, did not seem to be shedding any light on the situation, so in divine timing, I met a healer who was able to steer me away from my usual practices and into my emotional body. This man changed my life.

When the neck of my cervix was removed, I was sent to the hospital a second time for retesting, and I was told my womb would also have to be removed. After the operation, the doctors said, "The womb was not cancerous upon testing. This is very strange." I was saddened deeply by this at first, this unnecessary second surgery, but at the same time was given conviction for the power of shamanic healing, which would be my life's new path of service.

You see, what a lot of spiritual practices do, including the practices I was raised with, is tell us to meditate, come into our center and stillness, come back into love and light and transcend the darker aspects of our being. However, life happens, and our body starts screaming at us, "Look at this!"

I looked all right! Before and after my surgery, my eyes began opening in the dark, and I was feeling what was underneath my mask of a strong, empowered woman. I screamed, I cried, I remembered and acknowledged sexual abuse that had previously been blocked altogether from my memory. I felt rage where I had felt neglect. I felt my feminine as an out-of-control wild beast, I felt my masculine as a bully and a tyrant, and I felt my scared, alone little girl. I felt like this journey into the darkness would never end.

Little did I know that this dark time in my life was leading me to my life path: shamanic tantra—the energetic path and descending into the emotional body with breath, sound, and movement. It felt like I was coming home. This time, I was releasing trauma from my body by going *into* the body rather than *out* of it. Understanding things at a consciousness level was no longer the priority. Being totally present and totally out of control became my new practice. I began to come back to a body I abandoned long ago and live from my heart rather than my mind. I left my corporate job and became passionate about this new style of healing. Very quickly, I started training as a tantrica and working as a supporter on many tantra workshops around the globe, as well as facilitating my own.

As I journeyed in new directions, my marriage ended, and a new relationship began. I was being met in very new and exciting ways, which was very beautiful but also very difficult. It became like a spiritual soap opera—dramatic and emotional, love and hate, push and pull, leaving and coming back, monogamy and polyamory, wounds battling each other, personal and archetypal, tantric and multidimensional, deeply passionate and deeply destructive. It was very real and very raw. There were fires, tears, war, peace, rose petals, and plenty of thorns.

This relationship was undoubtedly bringing up more darkness in me than all the sessions, workshops, and trainings put together, which meant it was also the biggest catalyst for my growth. I had never experienced a love like this. It was an initiation into my sacred feminine where I was constantly faced with two options: complete destruction at the helplessness of having absolutely no control, or complete awakening through allowing the dark to birth more light. In the end, I realized that for this initiation to reach its full potential, I had to disentangle myself. The crucial key was when I decided to leave the crucible *for good* and put an end to that which was the most challenging thing I've ever had to do in my life. It was also the most empowering!

After leaving the relationship, I wondered who I was before I was diagnosed with cervical cancer … but I could not find her again. The little princess who was uncomfortable with her pain and who wanted to be rescued by a king was burned alive, and in her place was a woman who knew that she was her own hero and *that* is what would make her a queen. It was that part of me, the princess, that I grieved for a very long time—am still grieving at times actually. I also let go of the part of me that thought I was unlovable, the part that made me such an easy target. I love knowing that I deserve love. I love that I no longer turn crumbs into gold. I love that I now know how to ask for what I need and assert healthy boundaries.

My life pre-tantra seems unimaginable. Nowadays, I am living my authentic path with a man who not only totally meets me emotionally but who I can serve this planet with. He is a reflection of the hero or the masculine that I was forced to cultivate in myself if I was to heal the wounds within.

The trigger for this life transformation was undoubtedly my cervical cancer.

Thankfully, I don't live in fear of my pain or the unknown anymore. I walk with it now. I'm not afraid of anger anymore. I feel it and let it transmute into power. I no longer have my physical womb, but what I do have is the grace of all the lessons learned. Another great gift was that during an emotionally unstable relationship, which was the worst possible time to have a child but a time where I really wanted one, I was unable to. So not having a womb, in a way, saved me from myself. As my father always says, the universe gives you what you need, not necessarily what you want!

I look back at this time of my life as a cocooning. The most profound insight I've had from this butterfly stage of my life is realizing just how much energy I now have to be in service to the world. More than anything, being in service has been my greatest tool for growth. Really learning what it means to show up in love and presence. Also understanding how much easier it is to be in true service when energy is not being constantly drained by the endless drama of a dysfunctional relationship experience. It's frightening to think how much energy was being lost from me and distracting from my creativity, ease, and power. And guess what? I'm actually earning more than I was in my corporate role, consistently.

I'm still learning and growing all the time and helping others do the same … to go into their pain rather than avoid it to feel their grief, their anger, their frustration without judgment and release it out of the nervous system. To know that pain and pleasure are both as beautiful as each other, and both are always in the flow of life. The key is to not be attached to the pleasure and not resistant to the pain. To simply *be* ourselves in the multicolored spectrum of life—all of it. This is what tantra is. Tantra is life.

Paige's Story

We are all of us a mixture of flavors ... a soup of what it means to be human. Paige shares her experience of growing up living in the middle of worlds and how it has made her more beautiful.

My story …

*T*o bring the words I wrote about my experiences as an Afakasi half-caste Cook Island/ Italian to life. A short depiction of the obstacles that many mixed bloods go through when it comes to their culture. I hope that people who have lived through something similar can understand that and see how beautiful they are!

Paige

An Afakasi's Lot

Neglect,
The lack of respect;
Minimal, generalized judgment cast upon me,
An undermining subliminal,
I was criminal.
Inferior to my culture, it was snatched from me like a vulture hunting
her prey.
Summer days,
My hips would naturally away
To the sound of the ukulele
As they tried to persuade me
I did not belong because the shade of my skin.
My body shape too thin,
My grin
Revealing, kept teeth too white like the pale of my sister's skin,
The clothes we were in,
Too expensive for the life that many Polynesians choose to revel in.
Like my Italian heritage,
Mouth too big,
Like the house we used to live in.
I was ashamed of me,
Uncomfortable in this vessel that God made for me, drowning in a sea
of acceptance. Someone please save me!
But this did not break me;
This made me!
For during the journey toward my salvation,
I realized that we were never your *average*,
But continually subject to the savage opinions of the women who had
the same blood Running through their veins as my dad did!
But no longer am I a child,
Defenseless and fearing them,
For I am a woman of strength.
I am a Polynesian.
And just as I let my culture go,
I *can* take it back,
Because, like my education;

My Mana* it does not lack.
My arrogance nonexistent,
My Whanau's Kaha* is consistent.
And my art will reveal to you my persistence
To wear my culture like a crown with no resistance,
So hear this!
I am a beautiful woman with my Wairua* strong,
Healed by the depths and harmonies of traditional Maori song,
Binding our people together with an undeniable bond.
Kapa Haka,* the Siva,* the Hula—for all of these my soul sings.
So forever thanks to both my Mangaian and Samoan fathers for the good our culture does Bring.
See, I realized I never lost the right of access to Polynesia.
I nearly stood aside and watched it be criticized beyond measure.
Not only by outsiders but by those who were within,
My very own family,
The born-again Christian congregation;
My list, it does not end.
So I *choose* to take a stand with my passion now lit,
For my culture does not define me;
I define it.

* (Māori) In Māori culture, Mana is many things. It is honor. To have Mana is to have great authority, presence, or prestige. It is respect. Whanau is family; Kaha is power/strength; Wairua is Spirit; Kapa Haka is a Māori cultural performing group.

* (Samoan) **Siva** is a Pacific Island dance.

Bernadette's Stories

Bernadette is a being of the ocean and has spent much of her life at sea. The sea creatures know her. Dolphins come find her; they know a likeminded soul. Bernadette gave me two ethereal tales of womanhood, one of heartbreak and one of watching your child become a woman. Both were beautiful and worthy of being in this volume.

Photography by Kyle George

Rock the Boat

(A tale by Bernadette)

Something woke me.

Perhaps it was the moon.

Her face—round, clear, composed—is the first thing I see out the porthole when I open my eyes.

Clearly, she has been watching me for some time.

Inside my head, fierce words string together, forming sentences that continue to roll over and under one another, unfinished, like frayed thread.

Jay. Where are you?

I had begun to feel more and more like an intruder in their reminiscing, like I was somehow to blame for not being able to contribute to their stories of the good old times.

So this time, when Jay set off to see her, I had decided to hang back. He had not been disappointed, had jumped straight in the dinghy, the top of a new packet of cigarettes shouting loudly from his shirt pocket.

I had watched him row toward the shore, toward her house. Although he had faced in my direction, I knew he didn't see me. With each stroke of the oars, he had receded further away, until he slipped from my world completely.

I climb up on deck and stand at the bow. Stars contrast sharply against the predawn sky. And in the east, an otherworldly glow traces the hilltops, barely a whisper of daybreak.

Somewhere in the dark sea below me, the anchor holds fast to the seabed.

I look toward her house now.

The dinghy is pulled high up on the shore. Jay is nowhere to be seen.

I move to the stern and sit heavily on the aft deck, wrapping my arms around myself fiercely, as though this might keep me from breaking apart.

Feeling like I have nowhere else to turn, I lift my face toward the deepening blue of the sky, catch hold of my breath and wait, hoping for some kind of message to guide me through this new sea.

But there is nothing but space above me, a space that only seems to highlight even more my own terrible insignificance.

There are no clouds, no birds, no rainbows or stars. Just a sweep of sky so vast I feel as though I am falling upwards.

Before I realize it, a voiceless scream begins building, tearing at my chest.

It comes from somewhere so deep, so far away I don't even know its birthplace.

Unable to contain it any longer, I surrender angrily to the flood of despair. Tears fall like rain, and a scream with no sound erupts from my mouth like a vicious windstorm. I let it take me, driving me along in its urgency, carrying me precariously closer to something I don't yet understand, until there is no breath left in me.

Wearily, I stand, a damp pile of ashes where my heart should be.

A slow breeze breathes around my hair, murmuring softly of sea birds waking, of flower buds opening, of stars fading.

But the beauty of this day arriving is too much for me to look at alone, and I descend back down into the shadows below deck. Wrapping myself in a light blanket, I climb into a bunk. I switch on a lamp, fold my wings tight toward my heart, and wait.

"You *bastard*!"

My face flushes hot with anger.

Jay's image softens to a blur behind my tears.

My whole body shakes.

I am just as horrified by him as I am at myself; the ferocity of my words had erupted from out of me as if they had been coiled inside like a serpent ready to strike.

"I'm sorry, Bernadette."

I turn from him and look ahead, out over the wide Pacific Ocean, toward the last flush of light on the western horizon.

"I'm sorry," he repeats.

It is only minutes before my watch starts. Above us, the main sail trembles, holding the wind in a tight embrace. Stars have just begun to appear, arcing out over the vast seascape like sequins. It should have been perfectly romantic, but instead I continue to stand with my back to him, turning to stone.

Why am I so afraid to speak?

The wildfire of anger I had felt earlier was a fast-dropping anchor and taking firm hold in a bed of sadness. A rogue wave of loneliness surfaces, leaving me feeling I am only a fraction of myself.

Where did the rest of me go?

All of a sudden, trying to salvage our shipwreck becomes urgent. I feel desperate to stop the rot that continues seeping into our every day from billowing around behind me, from tainting the story we have already written together.

It can't have all been for nothing!

The volley of words that had tormented me the night before begin slowly rising. I roll them over in my mouth with my tongue, imagining how they will sound out loud.

I know I'm rocking the boat.

Then out of nowhere, an image of a little girl rises …

She is running, wild eyed, chasing her mother to the car.

In her mind, she is screaming, *Stop! I'm not ready for this!*

Then in a cloud of gravel, her mother accelerates out of the driveway, leaving her behind in her turbulence like a little moth caught in a storm.

Defeated, the small girl drops to the ground, a scream rising from the pit of her stomach, ballooning grotesquely until it peals from her mouth like a siren, louder and louder, with no end.

She drives her pain out through her mouth, trying to rid herself of all the hurt that has heaped up like hot molten smoldering inside her.

The sound of her own screaming reaches her vaguely, as though it is happening to someone else far away.

Then just as it is about to engulf her completely, she opens her eyes to see her sister standing over her, wide-eyed, pale.

"Bernadette," she whispers, "it will be all right."

Jolted back to my body as though I have fallen from a great height I snatch at the scream, tearing it off at my throat.

I could have laid there forever, but a feeling of profound shame motivates me to move.

I stand quietly. I have accomplished nothing. My mother is gone.

I vow never to raise my voice again.

I turn to look at Jay, waiting for me to accept his apology.

My voice snags painfully in my throat, and disproportionately emotional, I begin to cry with gusto.

He is quite stunned, and I can tell he is not happy at my meltdown.

I try desperately to pull myself together, but I feel lost, a foreigner in my own body, and the need to connect with him, to have him confirm I am still *me* and that I am still *good*, becomes unbearable.

For a moment, his fingers land gently on my arm like a rare bird alighting on a branch. The magnificence of the moment steals my breath, and then just as suddenly, he moves away from me and is gone.

"I am a complicated man," he says instead, as if that will explain everything.

And then, like a second shadow falling, my thoughts are carried on another riptide of memory, back to Egypt eight months before.

The man sits smugly across the room amidst the folds of his *gallibaya*, now far too close for my liking.

He has just finished proudly telling Jay that he has three wives, as though he were merely talking about having an extra helping of dessert.

I feel myself squirming uncomfortably but make room for a tiny flicker of hope; Jay will put him straight. There's no way Jay will give his approval. Jay would certainly not want to share me with anyone.

I raise my head and lay claim to the space I take up sitting on the floor of this man's house and watch for Jay's response. But instead, a smile tugs at the corners of his mouth, and he leans back in his chair. He looks so delighted, so proud, I think for a moment he is going to stand up and high-five him.

A flush of humiliation burns within me while Jay's words of approval fall around me heavily like stones.

But no one notices. Not only am I now invisible to this stranger, Jay also does not see me.

It is as though the room has cleared of dust, and I see myself sitting on the fringe of this conversation between two men, an object owned and on display, my pretty plumage simply only one design amongst many for the taking.

Jay had uprooted me from his heart, but somehow I was still captured.

How did I get here?

These unwelcome memories burn like fire in my belly, and I can feel the little-girl me still dangerously close to the surface.

I try telling her this is not the place for her, but she is not that easily convinced.

Instead she sits with me, silent, watching, waiting, wondering what I will do next, ready for fight or flight.

Wiping the tears from my eyes, I leave Jay sitting alone on the back deck and begin my watch.

I know it is time, time for me to find my voice, to rekindle my own fire, to follow the direction of smoke back home to myself.

I would need to rock this boat ...

On Motherhood

(A tale by Bernadette)

A man is in the house.

What if he is not really here to fix the lights?

I rise from the edge of the bed where I sit perched carefully on hot coals.

My breasts chaffed and swollen scream fire.

I lower myself painfully to the floor and pace, ears pricked, hissing

At the edge of the bed where my three-day-old baby sleeps.

I had entered through the portal into motherhood only to find I did not know where I was.

I knew only that this man would get nowhere near my baby.

She was three days old when we carried her, screaming, back home.

Her placenta felt heavy in its cardboard box as I carried it out to the trees at the edge of the bush by the house. I watched in silence as this thing that had sustained our baby while she grew in my belly fell in a wet, heavy heap, spent, into the hole we had dug at the base of a beautiful tree.

We walked slowly back to the house, and I cried. I knew this was supposed to mark the occasion of something truly beautiful. But I couldn't help feeling I had buried myself out there under the tree.

I felt an exhaustion that nothing in my life had prepared me for, a dull and heavy pain that pulled at every fiber of my being.

Wasn't I still meant to glow?

Worst of all, for the first time in my life I felt betrayed by nature. And that scared me more than anything.

Sequoia barely slept, and when she did, it was gossamer-fine.

A creaky floorboard in another part of the house or the whisper of air that moved to fill the space when you left or entered her room was enough to shock her into wakefulness. I could not find any pattern in our days and succumbed to living with her strapped to me in a front pack.

What was I doing wrong?

For the first six months of her life, she cried so loud and so regularly I could no longer hear the *piwaiwaka** calling from the low branches of the punga tree outside.

Was she homesick for my womb?

Sometimes I became afraid I was drifting so far away from myself I would never remember how to find my way back. Where once I had been a boat moving from shore to shore at the whim of the wind, I was now a tree on an island—sessile, my roots reaching deep into motherhood and the home while my branches strove desperately for light, reaching for the heavens, grasping at stars, toward understanding, acceptance.

Breastfeedingnappychangecryingbabyputtingdowncryingbaby pickingupagainbreastfeeding began to run like too much paint on a rainy day, and when I could feel the last of my former self slipping through my fingers, I phoned my mother.

I do not.

Know who.

I am.

Anymore!

And she came.

And held my baby, held me, and told me gently, "It will not be forever, Bern ..."

And just like a lighthouse, she sat in her presence, noninterfering, shining. Reminding me of the way home.

* New Zealand fantail bird.

Sequoia's tooth has fallen out.

She left for bed an hour ago with it in a little glass jar full of water.

I rummage through my treasures intent on finding something precious enough to give my eight-year-old daughter.

I pause, torn between a tiny paua shell and a small, colorful stone.

The fairies have left a paua shell for her before, and the colorful stone may have been given to me by Sequoia.

I decide to risk the stone, hoping I am wrong or that she won't recognize it. I drop it into an identical glass jar full of water that I will soon take to her room. It looks so unconvincing, I decide to sit it on top of a two-dollar coin.

This is rare.

We all know Sequoia's fairies don't leave money. They have always preferred to leave her gifts from nature, instilling in her that the simple, beautiful things in life are to be treasured above money.

The next morning, she holds up the stone, and I watch her examine it closely.

"This stone may be mine."

"Really?" I say, coming over to look at it with her. A caught-in-the-act feeling surfaces, and feeling nervous, I hold back an impulse to burst out laughing.

Instead I say, "Do you think there are cheeky fairies who hide things from people then return them in exchange for teeth?"

Sequoia smiles at the thought, then adds, "Actually, I'm not so sure I have seen this stone before. It might just look like one I had once."

Yesterday Sequoia had asked me if the Tooth Fairy was real.

I somehow managed to evade the question without feeling like a liar. She seemed to move on quickly, strangely refraining from demanding the truth once and for all. Almost, I thought, as though she didn't want to know.

Is it my imagination, or does she understand my dilemma?

I think of her precious little tooth tucked away in a safe place with four others not far from where we stand now, and I feel trapped.

Sequoia still has fifteen teeth yet to fall out. I thought that the whole Tooth Fairy thing would have been over before she was old enough to know it wasn't real! I did not see this coming. I can feel a mild panic rising.

What am I to do?

This just wont stick in another year! Then what will I tell her? That the Tooth Fairy had been real, but this year they didn't come, and so we had to step in? Or that the whole thing had been a trick all along?

Lately I have heard myself speaking a bit too loudly of magic and goodness, trying to convince her and perhaps myself that it truly exists. I have found myself wanting to follow her every move, my hands poised, ready to hold all that childlike purity in like slapping patches on a leaky bucket.

I suddenly feel unreasonably tearful.

If there is no Tooth Fairy, then what's left?

Sequoia has known from early on that Saint Nicolas was indeed a real person, but Father Christmas didn't come down our chimney to leave us gifts. This has been okay for all of us, but somehow I had needed fairies to remain a wonderful possibility for as long as possible.

But more than that, I can't bear the thought of Sequoia knowing we have lied to her.

Did other parents feel this way or was I being irrational?

After all, it was just the Tooth Fairy … or was it?

Beneath my inner turmoil lay something else, a nagging sense that something of profound importance lay wrapped up in all this.

My baby was gone!

The suddenness of her abrupt absence overtaking her presence was like a freight train had mowed me down. In waves, those trains would come, again and again. Relentless. Each time, I was held down until I could stand the sense of loss no longer, and a cry of anguish would be forced from my body. For a moment, a memory of childbirth flickered in the pit of my belly. But this was not the song of birth that was raging through my veins, that was ringing in my ears.

Behind each pummeling, I would surface breathless and aching to a dark, oppressive place where grief dwelt heavy and uncaring.

When I awoke, my face was wet with tears.

Beside me, my daughter lay sleeping, her breath making soft, easy sounds like a breeze through leaves. Indeed, time had stolen my baby from me, and here in her place slept a child. How would I endure the next loss of my child to young woman, and then young woman to adult?

Like butterflies landing my fingers reach out to touch her, the warmth of her skin melting away the last remnants of my terrible dream.

———

I had not been worried at all while she tried it on at home.

After all, it was just a bikini.

But as I watch her walk toward the water, oblivious of the male surfers approaching from the other end of the beach, I see her long limbs carrying her with an impossible gracefulness. I see her golden hair falling away below her shoulders, a woman's body budding just beneath her thin waist and small hips, and an uneasiness I cant quite define descends around me, making it harder to draw breath.

And as much as I want to rush toward her and clutch her to me tightly as if to ward off her inevitable growth into womanhood and the potential dangers that lie in wait for her there, I know by looking at her stepping off the sand and into the water that somehow my daughter has just outgrown my reach.

Kendra's Story

When you are a naturally giving person, it can be hard to ask for help; often you feel almost embarrassed to ask. Givers naturally take care of other people first. In this heartfelt and vulnerable sharing, Kendra explores with us a tragedy she lived through and how she found it so important to speak up for her spark of light.

$\mathcal{I}$ was fifteen years old, almost sixteen, and about to enter my first year of high school. My parents had rented a house at the lake over summer break, and my best friend and I spent almost every day playing beach volleyball and hanging with the other teenagers, soaking up our last few weeks of freedom. We'd talk constantly about what high school was going to be like. Parties, boys, and the volleyball team … it was going to be an amazing few years!

A few weeks before school was about to commence, we met a small group of boys from our soon-to-be high school. One particular boy took a strong liking to me, and within a couple of weeks we had officially become an item. I had my first real boyfriend! We were inseparable.

Like many teen girls, I had completely morphed into his life, and we became very codependent. Our isolation from other friends actually happened pretty quickly, and in the beginning, I didn't even notice so much. I went on all his family vacations and started to pull away from my own family. My parents had started to show some serious concern about our relationship. They could see the light in me shutting down, and they were worried about my constant need to make sure he was always happy. The isolation was progressively getting stronger, and I started to hear of various parties that happened over the weekend and realized the invites that I used to decline were no longer being made.

I started to feel an ache for that fire in my heart I used to have when I was connecting with friends and dancing into the night. At this point, I felt so insecure in those old friendships that I was never able to reach out.

My boyfriend became more and more withdrawn from the outside world after high school, and I became more and more insecure in every way. I felt like every ounce of energy I had emotionally, I gave to him. I was distant from my parents, no longer wanting to defend his outbursts toward them or me. I felt like no one understood! He was sad and dark … it felt like he was slowly falling deeper into a darkness, somewhere that I couldn't even find glimpses of light to grasp onto.

We had no idea what depression was. I just couldn't understand why he couldn't see how lucky he was to be strong and fit and able to do anything he wanted to do, and I would be there to assist him with any and all energy I had left. I didn't see just how lost I had gotten in the process. Sleeping beside someone, begging them to just talk to you until you've cried so much you have no more tears, and you lay staring at the ceiling, feeling completely raw ...

Five long years went by, and I had missed all of those teenage rites of passage. No May long camping trips, no parties, no one cheering my name as I walked up to get my diploma at graduation. My boyfriend was suffering from a mental illness I knew nothing about, and I was so deeply lonely it hurt physically, and I had cut off all vulnerable communication over the years with those that I loved. I had no idea what to do. I felt so lost.

Drugs were the next phase of his illness. They were a way of treating his symptoms, and he didn't always want to do it alone. In my mind, it was, *Okay do whatever it takes—if it makes him happy, even if it's only momentary.* I already knew at this point that I needed to get out of our relationship. But something just kept me staying. I just felt so incredibly awful to want to leave, like it was selfish, and I never wanted to cause him more pain or anger than he was already feeling.

Months went by, and I got a new job and finally a friend. It was such an amazing feeling to have a simple thing like a girlfriend again. It brought something out in me that had long been pushed deep down inside. I got brave and told him that I wanted to take a break. I knew ending things completely would be too hard, hoping that just maybe it could be easier this way. It was the most difficult things I have ever had to do, but I needed to fight for my life.

I went home and soon after got a call from him. He said it was an emergency and to hurry and come pick him up. He said he was pulled over on the side of the road not far from my home. I jumped in my car and sped over. He had overdosed on pills and needed to be driven to the hospital. A picture of my four-year-old self was stuffed up his shirt.

I was devastated ... devastated with guilt, devastated with the knowing that this wasn't going to be a breakup like any other high school couple. I was back in the relationship. In my mind, I was going to have to sacrifice my life for his. If being with him made him stay alive, then that was what I'd have to do.

I never told my family of his attempt ... I just didn't know how.

His family was now involved, which was a relief for me. After the overdose attempt, I was introduced to the world of depression. The disease that haunted our young lives for far too many years. I felt like a shell of the person I was when our relationship first started, when I was full of light and love. I still wanted to travel and do humanitarian work, but that dream felt like another distant life.

I can't recall what spurred it, but I decided I needed the support of my family if things were going to change. I was in the car with my dad, and it just came out. I told him that I hadn't been in love with my boyfriend for a long time and desperately needed out of the relationship but didn't know how to do it. My parents had been concerned over the years and tried to talk to me many times. Had they known what was really going on, they would have helped, but I had always shut them out. I knew my dad was relieved to hear this but wanted to tread lightly in the wake of my sudden honesty. He said he and my mom were proud of me and that I was making a good decision. I felt so relieved to be honest with my family and so grateful for their support.

I let his mom know that I needed to end the relationship, and she said that she knew this day would come. I knew that he was in good hands with his doctors and his family, and there was truly nothing left in me to give. I called him on the phone this time, as we had just had another fight and I was scared to do it in person. I told him that I would always love him but that this relationship was no longer good for either of us.

He responded with pleas of love, and when those didn't work, he used threats. That's when I knew I needed to get off the phone. I never shared the threats with anyone. I was too embarrassed.

I'm not even sure how long, as it's a blur, but over the next couple days or weeks, I got calls and letters of love and letters that were not so kind. But I was doing my best to get back involved with friends and family. I was even going to my first barbecue with friends. I had just walked into the house to get ready when the doorbell rang. It was two police officers. They asked me to sit down, and as soon as his name left their lips, I dropped to my knees. He had done it. He was gone.

My heart felt broken.

Had I done the wrong thing? Was I selfish to have left?

The answer is no. We were just kids who were up against a disease much bigger than we could have ever fought alone. Maybe if we had been more educated on mental illness, we might have been able to get professional help sooner. But I knew in the deepest parts of my heart that if I hadn't had the courage to leave, there was a chance he would have taken me with him. He was sick; this was not who he was and is not how I remember him. I remember the sixteen-year-old boy who liked racing bikes and me.

But I now needed to mend my broken heart, and walking around in his clothes and sleeping in his bed, as I was doing, wasn't going to help me recover. I knew that in order to heal, I had to throw myself into something greater than my own grief.

Two months later, I volunteered in an Amerindian village in Guyana. We were a group of youth without any religious or political association. We wanted to help those who were in need. We hung our hammocks in the Amazon just short of three months and made ourselves at home.

I felt honored to be welcomed, especially by the women and children. It was a healing time for me, to witness and connect with women who had experienced deep loss in their lives but somehow managed to live with such love and gratitude in their hearts. It also made me understand the importance of community compared to my first world home where many people suffer from loneliness and isolation.

I learned so much in those three months. Most importantly how to live compassionately, love wholeheartedly, and grow a community of friends and family that allows me to be my truest and most vulnerable self. I lived many years with so much love and friendship to give but no one to share it with, but I have learned if you keep projecting your inner light, your tribe will find you.

Over the next fifteen years, my life and heart have grown exponentially, and I continue to feel more connected to my spirit and the energy of the earth and those around me. I have an amazing husband who helps me feel safe and grounded while also feeling connected to my free-spirited nature.

My first experience with death was at eight years old when I lost my closest neighborhood friend to leukemia, and then losing my boyfriend in my teens has left me with a real awareness of how precious life is and that the only moment we are guaranteed is this one.

I had always wanted to be a mom and was so happy to bring two beautiful boys into this world in my early twenties. They are my yin yang boys, opposites and amazing in their individuality. They have huge hearts and are intuitive souls. I do my best to love them in a way that makes their spirit free to explore the world, nature, their emotions, their inquisitive minds, and within all of that, the knowing that they have two parents who love them unconditionally with open minds and open hearts.

As all couples do, we have come up against many challenges in our relationship. My husband has been battling Lyme disease, and I have had to find my way through anxiety. Sometimes you feel like you're losing the battle, but then you choose to fight for what your heart knows it wants. And for us, that was each other. So we put the work in, we get honest, and we talk.

We continue to pursue what our own inner hearts yearn for. Sometimes he needs to immerse himself in nature and completely disconnect from the outside world for a few days. Sometimes I need to go see a musician perform whose lyrics resonate with my soul. Or I plan a trip to a country I have yet to explore, to immerse myself in their culture and learn from their experiences. We especially love doing these things together or as a family, but with young children, that's not always an option. So when it's not possible, then we support each other in our individual experiences and adventures, knowing that in return we have a life partner who feels more at peace in their heart and mind because they are feeding their soul.

I have also just started my own clothing label, Wilken Jade Designs, with my business partner and soul sister. Our vision is to create organic, ecofriendly clothing that is made ethically and that you feel proud to wear. We also want to give back to programs that we feel passionate about. Our goal was to create something that wouldn't hurt the planet or the people who made it. To share this with the world and to use portions of the profit to help those in need. This is a work of love.

I no longer have a broken heart from what happened all those years ago; it has been filled with compassion, love, and understanding. I know that I have one more angel protecting me while I'm on this life journey

My light is back, and my heart is open.

Kendra x

Esther's Story

It always amazes me how often the people who have been through the most pain are the most generous. When you have experienced knees hitting the floor from pain, something big happens. Your heart grows and is better able to feel the vulnerability in the world around you, and you see where you can bring your warm eyes and heart to help others. This is Esther. Esther is heart.

*C*he doctor told me I had what looked like a five-centimeter cyst on my left ovary. After months of pain, I was finally booked in to have it removed.

When I woke up after the procedure, instead of feeling relief, the pain was excruciating.

The first question the gynecologist asked me was how old I was and whether I had any children. He explained that I had severe endometriosis and that what they thought was a cyst on one ovary was actually a condition called "kissing ovaries."

My ovaries were so full of the endometriosis that they were stuck together. It was inside my uterus and in the lining of my pelvic wall. It was coating my bladder and bowel. They had not been able to do anything because he needed to discuss my options with me first.

He said that they could try to clean it up, but he believed that it was so invasive that it would be back with a vengeance within six months. He recommended a complete hysterectomy—removing both ovaries and my uterus, effectively sending me into menopause.

In my mind, menopause was what happened to old women. I was forty and in the prime of my life—fit and otherwise healthy. I wanted a second opinion!

The next gynecologist told me he could possibly remove all the endometriosis, but it would mean two separate surgeries with months of chemical menopause in between. They would put me on a cocktail of drugs to stop my period so that it didn't get worse whilst I was waiting for the next procedure. And even then, the trauma to my reproductive organs would probably send me into early menopause.

My boys were eight and two and a half at the time. I had a husband who had been diagnosed with multiple sclerosis and a mother in the final stages of dementia, and we were in the process of buying our first home.

I *did not* have time for this!

I struggled with my identity as a woman and wife. If I had all my reproductive organs removed, did that make me less of a woman? Would I still be desirable and feel desire? Would everything dry up and shrivel and turn me into a wizened old crone overnight?

After weeks of soul searching, I decided that anything would be better than the pain I was in, so I would go ahead with the hysterectomy.

The procedure was booked for March 26.

On March 4, we moved into our new house and started making it a home.

On March 18, late at night, I got a call from the nursing home to say that my mum was not doing well and that I should come and see her.

Even though Mum was already in a coma, I am so grateful for that call, so grateful that I got to tell my mum in her last hours how wonderful I thought she was, how much I appreciated what she had done for me and what she had given up for me.

I am so grateful that I could tell her that it was okay to let go and that I was there holding her hand as she slipped away from this life, this world.

For the past few years, my mum had been a shell of her previous vibrant, passionate self, and I thought that I had gone through my grieving process already for the woman that she was.

But the pain of losing her physical presence, however diminished, was like a kick to the core—overwhelming, overpowering, and like my whole world had been tilted on its side.

The day my mother died, I had my pre-op appointment at the hospital. I broke down when I told the doctor what had happened and said that I would need to postpone the procedure.

On March 26, the day I was due to have the hysterectomy, I buried my mother instead. In the week after the funeral, the grief was crippling. I couldn't stop crying. When people called, I couldn't speak to them. She was my last thought at night, and dreams of her calling my name woke me in the early hours of the morning.

On April 2, I finally had the hysterectomy.

I had decided that I didn't want to take the HRT that the hospital and my doctor were suggesting. I would see if I had any menopausal symptoms and how bad they were. I thought I was invincible! A strong woman who could push through anything.

Within a month, I was a complete basket case—stress, grief, and menopause had joined forces to render me a complete nightmare! I was angry, sad, hot, itchy, tired, and impossible to live with.

I decided to opt for a natural form of HRT in the hope that it would get rid of all the symptoms. Within the next two months, all the physical symptoms had abated considerably, but I was still on an emotional roller-coaster ride and taking my family with me.

One morning, when I found my fist raised at my eight-year-old son, I knew it was time to get help.

I felt like I was standing on the edge of a black hole and that I could just take one step into the abyss and disappear. In my mind, I had become a bad mother and wife. I felt so far removed from the loving, happy, easygoing person I used to be. The doctor diagnosed me with depression and put me on medication.

From the moment I started taking the antidepressants, my mind was filled with thoughts of how soon I could stop taking them. I felt so ashamed and like such a failure. Why couldn't I just cope with life? So many people had it much worse than me. I knew I was blessed in so many ways, so I must be weak and pathetic to need antidepressants.

They helped though. Within a few months, I was feeling much calmer, and if not quite happy yet, I would say that I was content. I had started working part-time in an industry I loved, and things were definitely looking up.

I weaned myself off the antidepressants six months after I started them, the minimum recommended time. Within six months I was back on them. Dealing with a very sensitive and stressful family situation and increasing financial pressure, I could feel myself slipping back toward the abyss.

Again I felt the shame and stigma that so often comes with the diagnosis of depression. It was like a big, dirty secret that I couldn't share with anyone.

Thank God for my children; they saved me. The thought of turning back into that person who could raise a fist to her own child was what sent me scurrying back to the doctor. If not for them, I probably wouldn't have gone back; I probably would have succumbed to the pull of that black hole.

This time I told myself that I would stay on them for one year to give myself the best chance of lifting those serotonin levels and being emotionally stable through difficult times.

Despite the MS diagnosis, my husband was still working in the car industry when the GFC made its mark on the world. The car industry was badly affected with sales in prestige cars dropping dramatically. Our financial pressures increased, and we couldn't make our mortgage payments. The only thing left to do was to sell the house.

After months of ignoring the growing signs and symptoms of depression creeping back into my life, I had a complete breakdown.

One minute I was in the kitchen putting together a platter for my son to take to his last day of primary school, and the next minute I was walking in circles, howling, in the grip of a full-blown panic attack.

I couldn't catch my breath or talk. I could only weep and scream in anger and pain.

My boys watched it all unfold in bewilderment until my husband could take them to a friend's place. That friend called another friend to come and stay with me.

On the way to my house, that friend called the doctor and made an urgent appointment for me. When she got to me, I was still having difficulty breathing and talking, but she managed to get me dressed and to the doctor.

The doctor prescribed antianxiety tablets for immediate relief from the panic attacks that were engulfing my body and put me back on the antidepressants.

That night I managed to attend my son's primary school graduation despite the gnawing grip of anxiety in my chest and my gut. I refused to ruin this special night for him, and I was determined to never, ever, ever be in this dark place again!

During the following month, I started intensive counseling sessions, which taught me coping strategies to deal with difficult situations that triggered my depressed state.

I learned to recognize the warning signs and not to ignore them.

I learned to stop the negative self-talk, which only continued and exacerbated the cycle.

I learned to be gentle with myself and to make myself a priority.

I came to the realization that the house was just that—a house. If we had to sell it, so be it. We still had our family unit no matter where we lived.

I surrendered to everything good and bad that might come my way and made my peace with the outcomes, whatever they might be.

I gave up worrying about things beyond my control and started focusing on things I could do to change my circumstances.

I started doing hot yoga. I needed the physical, mental, and spiritual challenge that only this form of exercise can bring for me.

Over the next eight months, I became strong yet flexible in body and mind.

I had set firm boundaries, taken my power back, and was learning the art of detachment through Buddhist teachings. Most of all, I spoke my truth. I told my story, warts and all, to anyone that mentioned they were feeling down, that life was getting on top of them.

I hoped that would encourage others to seek help in whatever shape or form they needed to be whole again. I wanted to make people realize that they are not alone—that so many suffer silently with depression and anxiety, thinking they are weak and unworthy of help.

In all these ways, I healed myself of the scars that depression had etched into my soul. I had a lot of support and love from friends and family along the way. I have a lot to be grateful for.

I believe that everyone has a different path to the same ending; we are all searching for happiness and fulfillment in our lives. Some things are beyond our control, but the choices we make in how to deal with all the ups and downs that life throws at us are *always* completely within our control.

By the time my husband had his first major MS relapse in August 2011, I felt strong enough to cope with the demands this new crisis placed on my family. It was heartbreaking watching his physical and mental decline. It was gut-wrenching watching my sons see their father struggle with the worsening symptoms of his condition.

I cried me a river, but I did not fall apart!

He wasn't able to return to work, and another major relapse followed a year later.

Living with MS is a constant lesson in taking each day at a time; the nature of this condition means that some days are good and others are really bad.

My husband's strength, positivity, and optimism in the face of his own huge struggle have been a constant inspiration to me.

In these last five years, I have managed to keep my depression at bay. I have weathered the storm. My scars have made me strong, fierce, and powerful, and maybe that is the same as beautiful!

My message is this:

Ask for help when you need it!

Feel the shame if you must, but do it anyway!

Help others whenever you can but learn to say no if you are feeling depleted and lacking in energy.

Focus on all the blessings in your life but work on changing the things you are not at peace with.

Share your truth with others who show an interest—not only to help them but also to set yourself free of whatever is holding you back.

Most of all, reach for whatever makes you happy with open arms and a hopeful heart.

Love,

Esther x

Jayney's Story

It takes a special person to hold space when others are in deep trauma, face it all—the worst things—and be the calm anchor helping others find a way forward. Jayney's journey is a powerful tale, and it has helped her know how to help others when they are in the hardest of times. She is not afraid to share her vulnerable journey, and despite the plethora of scars life has thrown, her kindness and warmth have never left her.

*T*hinking of putting who I am into words and how I got to this point seems overwhelmingly complex.

I have many scars.

Some that I have always loved and others I spent years refusing to think about, terrified of letting them have some sort of power over me.

Although I have always been a great explorer of self and others, somehow I managed to convince myself that certain pain and suffering didn't deserve a voice.

It has been a long and incredibly challenging journey to find vulnerability in myself, something that still doesn't come easy. Why?

I never identified with who I was as a child, fat with Coke-bottle glasses and in all the "special classes." I never really fit in anywhere, was never really good at anything, but I felt so incredibly lucky and special. Maybe not at school, as kids can be so cruel, but in myself.

I never spoke a harsh word to myself or believed what they said. I attribute this to the most amazing people I ever met—my grandparents and also my loving parents and sister. My mum had no easy task raising me. I was not easy to understand, but she always saw my light and found me interesting.

How I never felt second best to my amazing ballerina sister, I will never know, probably due to her love and admiration for me. She would have to be my biggest fan, and I am certainly hers. She has always been the light of my life in the brightness and in the dark.

At nine years old, I started at a new school where I met a dear friend who profoundly changed my life by loving me, as well as a soul mate who made me feel cool for the very first time. If only the three of us knew back then what life had in store …

I have only recently admitted to myself that my first true scar happened at this time when I was walking home to my grandparents' house. I was dragged into an empty playground and raped by a filthy old man who used to hang around the school.

I found out years later that the same thing had happened to another friend of mine, although we never spoke of it until years later.

I remember sitting in the bath at my grandparents' house, rationalizing …

At least he didn't punch me. At least my parents don't know, as they would be really upset with me. At least it wasn't my sister! She wouldn't have coped.

I made the decision there and then that this man had taken a few minutes out of my life, and I wasn't going to give him any more than what he stole. I felt happy and resolved and took the long way home from school from then on.

Unfortunately, as a ten-year-old kid, I could have never understood that this decision would profoundly change who I was.

During this time, my parents were managing separation. My dad came out as gay, moved three hours away, and my mum re-partnered. For a while, we had been spending about a week with each parent, but when Dad moved, I experienced my first real heartbreak.

I felt a complete lack of control and was devastated. I wasn't adjusting well to my mum's new husband and felt completely abandoned by Dad.

I did truly want him to be happy but felt broken that as a ten-year-old girl, I wasn't enough to keep my dad with me.

———

Next minute, I was in high school, a prestigious school with none of my friends around me. Luckily, I soon found dance. Dance gave me my tribe.

Dancing was the first thing I ever felt good at, and everybody at dancing loved me because I was the sister of the beautiful ballerina that everybody aspired to be.

At thirteen years old, I had my last eye operation and lost the thick glasses as well as the puppy fat I had dragged around like armor my whole childhood. I became popular, especially with the boys, and started to feel on top of life.

High school was all about boys (or girls when they would show interest) and dance. I failed every subject every year and was certain that I was completely stupid academically. I never felt bad about it, but I never challenged the truth of this thought, so I limited many options.

At sixteen years old, I met domestic violence. For two years, I lived that victim cycle. I was living away from home and teaching dance for a living. I was so young. The relationship I had with domestic violence was a relationship of pain that sadly also provided me with a level of passion and obsession that was hard for me to walk away from. But walk away I did.

I was so happy when after years of bruising, I was finally free. My best friends were by my side all the way through. We were always family and always there to work through whatever life threw at us.

A few years of fun and many loose relationships went by before reconnecting with an earlier love. Our connection was undeniable, and the warmth and safety he provided was everything I could ever want.

Six weeks later, I left my life and took a one-way ticket out of town. Although I struggled so much with life in a new city, without my friends, we fell into a lifestyle that just became. It never suited me, but we got married anyway, and soon after, *she* arrived.

The whirlwind of my life, my greatest challenge who has taught me more about myself than anyone and who in many ways is my hero. My first and only daughter who has more strength and spunk than anyone I have ever met.

My baby girl's arrival brought much love and hope into my home and my family. By the time she was twelve months old though, I couldn't deny that the marriage was not for me. I did try to communicate how I was feeling, but low and behold, I found out that I was pregnant again.

I was resolved to play out my life as a wife and that I would somehow have to make it okay. I started to live through my dreams. I would look forward to night when I could picture my perfect life. When I could see her, my imaginary wife. When I could live the life I wanted. To escape the reality I had settled for. Back then, I convinced myself that this was just a fantasy rather than me looking and searching to find myself.

Then the phone rang. It was my dad saying, "I have melanoma."

My beautiful, darling dad ... please no!

The tears are streaming as I write this. I went to him and cooked, loved, talked, and told him, "Dad, I'm screwed. I'm married, pregnant, and gay."

He smiled and said to me, "When the time is right, be true to yourself and honest to all of those around you, and everything will work out fine."

At the time, I felt robbed by his simple reaction, but over the coming days, months, and years, this became my mantra.

Six weeks later, I held that beautiful man's hand as he slipped away. I was twenty weeks pregnant and stripped completely raw by grief. I knew when I rebuilt myself I would do it being true to myself and honest to those around me.

I returned to work after three weeks still so much in pain. I was working as a vet nurse and asked to assist the new vet at work. I walked in, our eyes connected, and there she was, the woman of my dreams. I didn't recognize her face, but her energy told me that she was here and everything was going to be okay. I felt suddenly at home and felt fully in my body and more myself than ever before.

We were inseparable from that day. Weeks later, I gave birth to the most magical being who had been missing from my life. I don't have words for the love or connection between us, but it is certainly something.

Weeks after that, I moved out to be with her. So many people have asked me about this part of my scar story as if it was just some scandalous affair worthy of harsh judgment and gossip. The truth is that it was just so sad, heartbreaking, such soul-disturbing pain for all of us.

It hurt many people, but my life and love was just beginning, and so it did with my baby and toddler and my love. She supported me to go to university and chase my dream of becoming a paramedic. University? I never even finished school or passed anything, but she pushed me, believed in me, and a few years later, I graduated Dux of my class.

Crazy!

So life. Looking back on it all. Who am I?

Am I the fat kid with the glasses? The teenage slut? The domestic violence victim? The woman that left her marriage for another woman? Am I really that person?

Or am I the person at work as a paramedic who has stood trying in vain to bring a baby back to life? Am I the person who cuts down a hanging soul and reads through suicide notes trying to understand. The best friend, the sister, the daughter, the mum?

No. I'm not really any of these. I am simply a spirit enriched only by rawness, real, truth.

The good, the bad, and the indifferent.

I want to experience *real,* and if there is *connection,* I want to live that for five minutes or fifty years. That's what I'm about.

Love lights me up. Any love. All love.

It's just what life is to me and what I will spend a lifetime practicing and hunting for, being open to.

All forms of divine love.

Sami's Story

One day, I was working with Sami on the table at Angels Rest while her daughter played with the blocks I had in the waiting room. Bella came quietly to me and climbed gently up onto my lap. Putting her hands over mine, she said, "It's right here." I could feel the healing power from Bella's tiny hands guiding me where on her mother's body needed releasing and support. Watching those tiny hands crisscrossed with scars over mine, I knew I was in the presence of a gifted healer. This is a lovely story. Enjoy.

ntuitively, I always felt I would have three children. When I met my husband fourteen years ago, I knew I had found my soul mate. I had found someone very special, someone I felt had the same values and beliefs as myself. I am so fortunate to have met such a caring and supportive man.

We had just relocated in late 2009 for my husband's new position with a mining company. We had planned to live in this smaller town for three years, but things changed very quickly.

Our eldest son had started at pre-prep for school, and with our youngest son at daycare one day a week, I felt like it was time now for me. Time to be doing something for myself. I thought of doing some volunteer work and that the hospital would be a good place to start. I had this urge that whatever work it would be, it had to be worthwhile, helping people. I realized I was now at the stage at my life, thirty-nine years old, and needed to find my purpose—what I should be doing with my life and career. I guess I felt a little lost.

We started trying for our third child, and to our surprise, one month later I was pregnant. With two active boys already four and three, the thought of another child scared me, but I was ready. I had always dreamed of having a baby girl, but I was certain I was carrying another boy. I could really see myself with the three boys driving me crazy running around. I just couldn't imagine myself with a daughter. It was a wish I just thought would not happen.

When I did the routine neck/blood scan at ten weeks, I never gave it any thought. I still remember lying on the bed having the ultrasound done and looking at the baby on the screen and feeling something wasn't quite right. I didn't know what it was, but now I know it was my intuition. I didn't say anything to my partner, and as time went by, I forgot about this thought. I had done this nuchal screening procedure in my previous pregnancies with my two boys and just thought it was routine, and I guess we never really discussed the what-ifs.

When the GP called me and asked if I could come and see him, I was a little worried. My husband was offsite at work, and both boys were at kindergarten, so I headed off to the clinic alone. My previous pregnancies had both been easy with no complications. So sitting there, nervously waiting for the doctor to talk, it was a shock when the words were blurted out, "You have a one in two chance of your baby having Trisomy 21."

I felt like I had been kicked in the belly. I listened and didn't say a word until what felt like ten minutes but probably was only ten seconds. I stopped the doctor from going any further with the conversation by putting up my hands. He wasn't going to tell me his thoughts. I just needed to run, run as fast as I could out of that room and get my boys and get home.

My husband flew home that night. We cried, and we talked and cried some more.

The next couple of weeks were so emotional and stressful for us. I knew I couldn't terminate this child, but I was so scared of how it would affect our lives. We knew with having a child with Down syndrome that he or she would be delayed in their learning and may or may not have a number of health issues, anything from heart problems, digestion, bowel … the list goes on and on. On the other hand, we also knew that our unborn child, just like our boys, would one day be able to talk, walk, read, write, go to kindergarten, school, and one day live an independent life. How could we terminate this child?

We decided to go ahead with a CVS procedure at twelve weeks. This procedure would confirm within twenty-four hours if our child had Down syndrome. I needed to know. Being such an organized person, I needed to start reading books and using the Internet to research as much as I could. To get my head around this, and we both needed to accept our baby for who she was going to be, and I could get on with having a positive pregnancy.

Off we went to hospital for the CVS procedure. The needle was inserted into my stomach, and I still don't like to think of that intrusive feeling I experienced. I would go through childbirth again instead of having this needle inserted into me. I was terrified it was going to miss and hit the sac and kill my unborn child. I couldn't take my eyes off my husband; we locked into each other's eyes and prayed for our baby.

Twenty-four hours later, I received a call at home.

"Your baby has an extra chromosome, and it's a girl."

Blurted out without thought, and again I was on my own. They had told me that we would be called into the office to get the news; however, it was a phone call with no support around me. I can't even begin to explain the pain I felt. The noise that came from deep inside of me was primal, something I had never heard before and hope not to again. Now I know it was a cry of grief for the perfect girl I had always dreamt of. I cried that I had been blessed with a girl, and I cried for the child having Down syndrome.

We then had our nineteen-week scan at the local hospital. The ultrasound showed that our daughter who we had already decided would take my grandmother's name had two holes in her heart. We were given abortion information, but no one discussed with us about proceeding with this pregnancy. I was nineteen weeks pregnant and already loved my child just as much as my two boys.

I saw the look in my husband's eyes as he watched the screen. There was devastation when we saw the holes. I just had this numb feeling and kept saying, "She will be beautiful, and it will all be okay." I needed to reassure him that it *was* going to be okay. *Yes she will have Down syndrome, and yes she will have a heart operation, but she will be okay! She is our daughter, and there's nothing stopping me from doing everything I can to make sure she is okay.* That's when the lioness took over; no one was going to take our girl away.

There was no way I was losing my girl! I am a believer that what you are given is part of your life's journey. Everything is just meant to be. I felt strongly that if we had chosen to abort Bella, it would have destroyed me and maybe our marriage. I am sure my heart would never have healed.

An inner strength that day came over me as my husband and I held each other outside the hospital. I told him and told myself that it would all be okay. I just kept saying inside and out loud, "She will be beautiful, and we will get through this."

At twenty-seven weeks pregnant, we relocated back to where my extended family lives. My pregnancy was gentle. I had the usual nausea and tiredness for the first twelve weeks, the same as with the boys, and then I felt great. I embraced my pregnancy and listened to meditations about meeting my newborn baby. I didn't know how I would feel when I first saw Bella, but I already knew she would change our lives and she would be beautiful.

Bella was born only one week early on the tenth day of the tenth month in 2010 and a healthy eight pounds, two ounces.

Bella's birth was textbook—waters broke, and two hours later she was born naturally. I will never forget when they passed her up to us. Her beautiful, big eyes stared deep into mine and then across to her father's. I was lost in those eyes … a moment I will never forget.

In the past five years, our Bella has undergone heart surgery, hand surgery, eye surgery, and two sets of grommets in her ears.

People have said, "You must ask, 'Why me?'" I have never thought this or asked this question. From the start, I always knew that this was the baby we were meant to have in our family, in our life. This is just the way it's meant to be for us. How could I ask "Why me?" when we have been blessed with such a happy, gentle, loving human being, and we made her!

Without having Bella, we as a family wouldn't have had the courage to move again interstate to a home that is everything we have always dreamed of. We now live on three acres of land with chickens, a veggie garden, and room for the kids to explore where the sun shines almost every day and a beautiful supportive community surrounds us. We are living our dream and hope for bright futures for all our three children.

Thanks to Bella, I now have a Flower Essence healing business, and I feel like she has given me the chance for me to the person I'm meant to be. She makes me a better person.

I sometimes feel she is the one looking after me, as she tells me often, "Mum, be brave, okay!"

Nikki's Story

A couple of years ago, I was thinking about writing this book and attended a Hay House writer's workshop in Sydney. Nikki sat next to me in the front row, and we connected immediately. She told me of her passion for writing children's books that were healing for kids. When the idea began floating around for Made Beautiful by Scars, Nikki was one of the first people to send in her story.

aving a baby wasn't going to change me. The baby would fit into our lives, and I would be such a wonderful mamma. Everyone who had seen me in the company of children knew that. I was going to continue my social life, going out, and my sporting life too.

Yeah right!

The moment my firstborn entered the world changed me forever. I knew that she wasn't "mine," that I was blessed to have the opportunity to guide this little person to be the best she could be. She kept looking, unblinkingly into my eyes. I felt so uncomfortable being seen. Yet I knew that I wanted to be everything for her.

All my parenting theories and extensive experience with other people's children went out the window in that instant. I knew that I had to carve out my parenting to suit her growth and, as I later discovered and am still discovering, my own growth.

As I struggled over the next few years, two messy miscarriages and another healthy baby boy later, there was no end to the advice of well-meaning people in my life attempting to help me find some kind of status quo.

Deep down I knew that I didn't fit that model anymore. That I wanted to be the best parent I could be. I wanted for my children that which I didn't have—opportunities, life pleasures, all of it. My children were worth it. Weren't they?

Somewhere in my quest for parental and family perfection, I lost me. There was nothing left. I reached a point when I couldn't give any more. I couldn't be the person my now ex-partner had met. I was failing in how a parent "should" be in the eyes of people I loved and had trusted. I was completely sleep deprived and emotionally depleted from breastfeeding both baby and toddler and from holding my shit together, being available for others' expectations. Trying to be "normal."

Until I had a wake-up call.

It was a wake-up call I could no longer ignore. There had been many others over the years. I hadn't taken any notice of them. I had made excuses. I fed the wolf of insecurity. Living by others' life rules. My self-esteem was shot, and I didn't know who I was, what I wanted from life. I didn't even know what made me laugh or feel good about myself anymore.

There was nothing left.

This wake-up call showed me that I didn't want *this* for my children. That I didn't want them to grow up thinking that *this* was how you behave or that *this* was what they deserved. They definitely deserved more than *that*. It reignited my spark to guide my children to be all they could be. Somewhere deep inside, I knew I needed to step into who I was even if I didn't know how. These children deserved a better life.

After making big life changes, it took me a further eighteen months to realize that *I deserved better* too.

And the life changes kept coming. Four house moves, including a stay in a women's refuge, two preschoolers in tow, one in cloth nappies—hey, I was saving the earth one cloth nappy at a time—until I found a secluded spot to call home. I loved our little space, and we made it our haven for three and a half years.

During that time, I dug deep, under the house, in the garden, and further inside myself. A work redundancy package was offered, and I accepted. I knew I couldn't make myself have a passion for the work I was doing, and I was no longer willing to face the city commute and the endless organizing to get two children to school and daycare and myself on an early train. Another job had been offered in a different department. I had been feeling that I couldn't keep facing negotiating or justifying why I had to arrive early so that I could leave work early and handle colleague resentment that I was working a different schedule.

So without any further plans or direction, I'm not sure who was more surprised when I opened my mouth and the words tumbled out. "I'll take it. I'll take the redundancy." So began another journey to find what I loved doing and my next step.

The evening of my last day of work, I was buying something for dinner. As I paid at the self-serve checkout—in no mood to talk to anyone—tears streamed down my face. How was I going to make this work? Where was my next paycheck coming from? The voice in my head said, "You will never need to worry about money ever again." More tears. I knew I just needed to keep noticing the signs and following the breadcrumbs.

Back when I started making changes, I looked everywhere for help. I saw three health professionals. I knew I needed to find activities that I might like doing and rediscover things that I used to like. A deal for a month of yoga landed in my e-mail inbox, and on a whim I started going. I sought help in alternative therapies and stumbled across meditation.

My journey to rediscover me—stronger every day.

Recently I sent all my paperwork to my accountant. This was the year I tied up many loose ends. I had sold all my investments that I had allowed someone else to invest (with my money) on my behalf. The financial losses were more than what many would put as a deposit on a house—approximately three years' salary. When the phone call came that the accounts were done, I was to be another $285 out of pocket (after the tax rebate) for the privilege of having that part of my life over. As I walked down to the beach, processing another financial loss, I let the anger roar through me. I ran into the water screaming, "I wash my hands of you," physically scrubbing my arms like a surgeon. I kicked the waves. I shouted obscenities at the ocean. The waves drowned out my voice. Between each wave as the sea receded, I felt it washing away the past. Through my incoherent swearing, I screamed, "I hate you." And that's when it hit me. I didn't hate anyone else.

It was me I had hated.

None of the swearing coming out of my mouth made sense. At all. Then through my sobbing came uncontrollable laughter from deep inside.

That was the moment that *I* "got it."

There is only one person who can set limits for me. There is only one person who can put my needs first. There is only one person who can take responsibility for what I allowed to happen.

Because the moment that I took responsibility for my part in my relationship was the moment it changed. Forever.

People "get it" or they don't. The people who get it are often the ones with their own life scars and major changes they've faced. I have spent my life looking for validation in others. I love my friends for who they are, and I more often than not put them first. I learned sacrifice and to not be selfish. So when I thought that I needed my friends to help me through my tough patches, where were they?

Through selflessness, where was I in all of that? I dug deeper. Who I am is still emerging, and it has been a scary process at times. To throw off the shackles of what my tribe expected that I was good at and how I should live my life. What the mob is doing has never really attracted me, yet living with bullying made me yearn for acceptance. Needing acceptance from others only plunged me deeper into an abyss of self-hatred, a feeling that I was never enough. Never fully accepted by others because there was always something different about me.

I was a living victim, guilty of abandoning myself in my need to please others. A victim of others' selfishness because I had allowed myself to continue being self-*less*. Many people just don't understand why you're making changes or will slip away from your friendship circle. Maybe your situation makes people fear that it could be them. And that's just too scary. On the flip side, wonderful new friends came from "nowhere" as I was open to the flow in and out.

Now when I feel fed up or impatient or anxious, I bring my thoughts back to what I need for right now. Sometimes, that means creating some space for myself—like having an early night or going out for dinner so I don't have to face cleaning up. Or it could be opening a tin of mixed beans and a tin of chopped tomatoes, mixing them together and calling it "soup" for dinner. Or letting the children run naked on the beach so I don't have to wash their wet clothes.

I focus on being the best mum I can be to my two children and finding balance. This is key for me. I am teaching my children to go with the flow and to resolve issues. I don't need to be right. I just don't live in my mistakes. I ask a lot of questions, of myself and of my children. The main one is, "How could we do this differently next time?" Taking the pressure off myself allows me to be the perfectly imperfect parent and the imperfect me. And that is truly humanly perfect!

Don't give up on yourself. You're the only person you need to live up to.

And you deserve that freedom.

Keezia's Story

A fellow Kiwi, Keezia and I bonded at her hair salon in Brisbane. She is a very wise soul, someone who has lived a rich and sometimes deeply painful life in the time she has been on this planet. Keezia's salon has the most amazing energy. For those who are lucky to connect with Keezia, they leave feeling heard, seen, and beautiful. She really is a very special human being.

s a child, pain is a scratched knee or a stubbed toe. Boy does pain feel different now that I'm a grown-up. Life seemed so much simpler then when I was a small child, carefree, riding bikes or embracing a mother's hug.

I was seventeen when my mother went missing at sea. Mum and her partner had sailed from the northern part of the South Island in New Zealand en route to Rarotonga. They had set out on a journey of a lifetime, of adventure and excitement. Verona always had that passion and zest for life in her. I think, as my sister and I grew older, she felt she could finally allow herself the opportunity to explore that part of her free spirit, let go of mother-guilt and be the free being she really was. Unfortunately, it was to be her last adventure.

It's strange how we can manage to block parts of our subconscious that we'd rather forget. It is just so much easier not to face pain head-on. Being teenagers when our mother died, my sister and I headed down different paths. Mine included partying—a lot of it. And I watched my sister settle into an intense relationship to find some form of safety. We could barely stand to be around each other. Her pain reflected in a mirror image of mine. Our relationship grew worlds apart. The one thing we shared in common during that time was that we were both using strong outside influences to try to fill a void. The void that was a huge hole in both our hearts—one that still remains.

The saying is true, you know; you never know what you've lost until it's gone. Even to this day, my eyes wander to families; a simple gesture of a mother telling a child they've done a good job can leave my heart with a stabbing pain. There is no stronger connection than that of a mother to child, a bond that cannot be broken. But why? Why did this pain have to happen to our family?

I believe in karma, but I also believe the universe has a divine plan. I think I used to play up on the fact that I'd experienced pain. Nobody could possibly know or understand what we'd gone through. We were special, and I felt it demanded to be acknowledged. A huge realization for me was that everyone in this world has pain. Nobody's pain is any less important or any more important. And it's okay to cry, to make mistakes, to get hurt and hurt others around you. I know I did a lot of those things. *A lot.*

Experiencing pain has helped me to step back and see that when others act out, there may be a reason. Nobody behaves badly without reason, and I believe deep down most want to be a good person to others.

I can't say it's been an easy ride, but my sister and I are in the best space we're ever been right now. She's my best friend, and we have each other's back. As I write this, I am planning to head off on an adventure Mum would be proud of—a great walk on my own through Spain, La Camino, a sacred journey where I expect to gently lay down so much more of my pain and heal my heart. I appreciate what this adventure is triggering for my family, but by allowing my free spirit to roam, I will free myself and her from those worrying feelings and give us all back our freedom and joy of adventure.

To mark the ten years since we lost our beautiful mum, my sister and I traveled to a very sacred place in New Zealand called Separation Point high above the ocean to say a releasing ceremony of great love for her. The rain, wind, and everything Mother Nature had decided to join us there where we were going to throw the ashes of letters to Mum into the ocean. We definitely felt Mum's sense of playfulness traveling with us. If we were planning on being serious the whole trip, she had other plans.

We traversed to the point via water taxi. It was a roller coaster on water, and I felt lucky to still have my breasts attached after that journey, even in a sports bra! Rain and strong wind blew our backs and fronts. As we anchored, a magnificent rainbow played over our heads. We felt Mum smiling at us.

As we began the climb, my rain poncho hit a wind gust and nearly flew me sideways off the cliff. My sister came to the rescue, tied it between my legs, and we were in stitches of laughter. We knew there was a colony of birds at the point. My sister has an irrational fear of birds, and as sounds of enormous cawing got louder, she refused to go any further. I told her, "We haven't come all this way for bloody nothing!" and she bravely kept on. It turned out the bird sounds were fake, a noise recording by the conservation people to help build up the bird colony.

Mum's sense of humor was with us, having the last laugh. Standing in the pouring rain and wind, scattering the ashes of letters we had written to beautiful Verona was a moment we will never forget. Through the laughter, the tears, the crazy wind and rain in our eyes, we got to say a loving and deeply healing farewell.

To overlook the ocean and landscape of the place Mum adored, I found it so hard to stay mad at the ocean. The sea had taken my mother's life away, and I realized how much anger I had held toward it. I couldn't stay angry. How could I? Knowing how much life it creates. It is so incredible.

I have now forgiven the sea.

Although it has been a decade, the pain still spikes, but I allow it and don't try to push it aside. I allow it to evolve. The anger has left.

Pain demands to be felt and moved through, and Lana and I have done a lot of work on that. Otherwise you just put a big old Band-Aid over a crying wound. A blessing for us is to know that we are loved by our mum eternally. She may have moved into a different room, but I often feel her adventurous spirit with us.

This scar of grief made me a woman overnight, a lioness, strong, sometimes tough but powerful. I have sometimes struggled with trusting love and opening my heart to its fullest. Or to allow myself to get lost in deep love in case it takes me on a dangerous journey, but I do know how to love and hold space for people in a way that offers great and deep care. I know how to really see others.

I named my successful hairdressing salon Verona after Mum, and it holds her beauty, her vitality, and her joy. My sister and I have worked here together, and for those who come here, they leave feeling heard, cared for, and beautiful. It is a vital, joyful place, and it holds Verona's playful energy. I know she would have been so proud of her special girls.

From my legacy of loss and the pain of losing my beautiful mother, I have learned to cherish my relationships with others. I have some very special people in my life, and I do not hesitate to let them know how much they mean to me. They feel heard by me, are met by deep presence. I am not afraid to say, "I love you."

My scar of grief has taught me to be a richer and deeper human being who appreciates that everyone has his or her scar to bear in life. Being comfortable with your scar, your pain, allows healing. It allows the scar to soften around the edges, become less raised and angry. It allows wisdom, depth, and a deeper appreciation of life … and love.

Don't let pain build up and create a weight on your shoulders. Be vulnerable with those around you. Embrace your scar and love it into a gentle walk to healing.

Feel the pain and walk through. It will heal you.

Love,

Keezia xoxo

R.I.P Verona Mary Hunt
1959–2005 Lost at sea x

Lou's Story

Lou came to Angels Rest, and I saw in those eyes a profound female wisdom and an incredible ability to see truth. After a session that evening, Lou felt this poem run through her. It arrived just before midnight. This is my favorite kind of writing creation. When you just let the words run out your fingers onto the page, they are real, they are fierce, they are powerful.

Scars
On your skin,
Your heart,
Your soul.
Scars are who we are.
The depth with which we choose to recognize them
Shifts and moves with time.
Our scars are many things.
They are
Hurt, despair, loss, physical injuries.
The skin heals,
But the memories, pain, and rejection live on.
Illusion, confusion,
The highs and lows,
Sleep then insomnia,
Making tidy excuses,
Loss of self-control,

The realization that I am me—strong and bold.
Time to stop telling the story.
No more hiding away, licking my wounds.
Letting go of the self-doubt.
That story …
It's doom and gloom.
Scars …
Feeling that I'm not enough,
Scars that he or she inflicted upon me and mine.
The wounds are a reminder not to go there,
But are they that bad?
Scars are part of our journey.
Touch and feel them.
Love and learn from your scars.

Be thankful for the blessings offered.
Scars are embedded in your soul.
As you move through the years,
Scars always carry a story that must be told.
Speak, act, and make a difference in this world.
Knowing that everyone you meet has a story and a scar,
Love one another.
After all,
We are who we are,
All beings seeking love and connection.

By Lou

Flawed Human

by Veronica

I am
Flawed human,
Stitched together with loving intention.
The light weeps through the cracks,
The knots,
The rusted parts,
And over time
Bathes them,
      Soothes them,
          Eases them,
              More and more.
I no longer ignore the damage,
Turn my head away,
Wrap my coat tighter
As I once did.
A smiling armor
Looking for a place
Where I could
      Arrive
          Into knowing
              All the things …
But instead
I have learned
That I know so very little
And to wrap
The roaring lost parts
In warm loving arms.
Sing to the dark places softly
Like a baby in arms;
Rock and heal,
Rock
      And heal
          Patiently …

I know
This is a lifelong journey.
The wounds have made me alive,
Made my heart deepen
With warmth
And compassion.
Each scar has helped shape me
To know life,
To know my brothers
And sisters,
    Their gifts
        And their dark places,
            All of it beautiful.
The cracks have helped me
Hold others more gently,
Murdered judgment
And criticism,
Freed me from hate
To lock eyes
And see sacredness
Hidden beneath gnarled branches
And creaking armor
    Is pure.
To see hope
Wash
Through hidden places,
Scour the depths of your pain,
Gives me greatest joy.
To see you drop your fists
And open your heart
To trust.
And allowance of all that lays hidden within
    Is superb freedom.
We are here to remember
Our divine male,
Our sacred female,
Beautiful, flawed selves within.
Stop the ego's mouth
    And be kind
        To ourselves
            And our world.

NOW, MY FRIENDS... YOUR STORY

*L*ovely Kate, who contributed to this book of scar stories and took some spectacular photos for it, sat over coffee one morning and gave me a beautiful image of what this book meant to her.

She said that for most women, we wear a heavy garment, a coat that we belt our scars beneath. As the scars get uncomfortable, we pull our coat in tighter, create more knots in the belt, so that we can hide our pain and appear more appropriate in the world. We compete with other women, so we can't ask for help to unknot these heavy and restrictive bonds over our beauty.

With the belt being so tight, it can be hard to see the gifts and wisdom that come from our scars, a deep knowing that so many others could benefit from.

My hope is that this book will give those who read it the opportunity to throw down their belts and their coats and heal their scars once and for all. This book is only the beginning. New stories are coming in to www.madebeautifulbyscars.com every day from women and men and even boys and girls, sharing their truth, sharing their light.

Each of the women who wrote for this book found new healing and personal power in sharing their tales. For each it was confronting to take off the belt, ease the knots, and say *all the things* publically, but we did it—we did it anyway.

Then something wonderful happened. As excerpts of the book were posted up online, women and men from all over the globe came to support those who were bravely sharing their tales. So many comments saying how grateful people were, what these stories meant to them, how it healed them too. Sharing vulnerable truth offered freedom and a release from competitive energy between women. It helped men open into vulnerability and warmth.

In poured the love.

Made Beautiful by Scars is a movement. One that has created a safe place for people to share the gifts they now live after walking through some of the most challenging experiences in their lives. Here you can be heard, held, and supported so the coat can fall to the floor. No meanness, no trolls invited, only care and support.

I love the idea of women and men being spectacularly free, of knowing how wonderful it is to no longer carry their scars hidden from the world. To know they are beautiful, powerful, valuable.

When it comes to your scar story, know this, and I mean it …

You can't do a bad job of writing your story.

Only you lived it. Only you can tell it.

So if you feel called to un-belt and drop your coat to the floor, come and share your wisdom with us at www.madebeautifulbyscars.com

Be it a piece of art, a poem, or a few pages of story, share your tale and heal your tale. Get ready though to own your story—and I mean *all of it.*

This is not a forum to blame those who may have caused your scars. You need to own that life scar experience and make your focus what you now know, what we can all grow from, what takes you into hope and new strength and takes us into this learning with you.

Be brave, lionesses and lions!

Be fierce and true.

You are valuable.

So much love,

Veronica

Made Beautiful by Scars is a revolution. We have been taught to hide our scars, move past them, and tuck them away. Not anymore. There are profound gifts in life's darkest challenges, gifts that we all can be empowered by. This book captures raw stories from twenty-three women who have faced all types of life scars and been made stronger, more powerful, aware, and real as a result.

Meet Kate—
Photographer,
Mother,
Healed of cancer,
One of our amazing
stories in *Made
Beautiful by Scars*

Kate Cornfoot Photography

From this book comes the *Made Beautiful by Scars* movement. Join Us! Share your story. Heal your story. Heal other women and men. Show them scars are beautiful, that none of us are here to be perfect. We are here to experience life and love our way through it!

www.madebeautifulbyscars.com

Printed in the United States
By Bookmasters